Brutal North

With many thanks to all the people who have made this book possible in these difficult times: Hannah MacDonald and Charlotte Cole at September Publishing, Guy Marshall and Dominic Hands at StudioSmall, Matthew Steele for his diligent work on the building captions and Russell Bell for his excellent maps. I would also like to acknowledge the kindness of all the people I met in the North of England whose assistance allowed me to take many of the photographs in this book. Finally, my family has always given me much encouragement and the support to keep going when things were hard, thanks always to Géraldine, Felix and Stella, and Colin and Jenny.

Simon Phipps

Matthew Steele would like to thank Richard Brook, Angela Connelly and Christopher Marsden.

First published in 2020 by September Publishing

Design by StudioSmall
Maps by Russell Bell
Building Information by Matthew Steele

Credits
P.011 cover of 'Outside The Trains Don't Run on Time' / 'He'd Send in the Army' by Gang Of Four, EMI Music Publishing Ltd, 1980
P.013 cover of *Grotesque (After the Gramme)* by The Fall, Rough Trade – Rough 18, 1980, cover credit: Suzanne Smith
P.013 lyrics from 'The N.W.R.A.' by Craig Scanlon, Mark E Smith, Stephen Hanley, from *Grotesque (After the Gramme)* by The Fall, Rough Trade – Rough 18, 1980
P.016 screengrab from *The Pacemakers: Dan Smith*, Central Office of Information, 1970

Printed in Lithuania on paper from responsibly managed, sustainable sources by BALTO print

ISBN 978-1-912836-15-4
10 9 8 7 6 5 4 3 2

Contents

The promised land of the South recedes in the rearview mirror, a distant fast-diminishing horizon where infantilised, cosmetic office blocks of glass and steel with nicknames such as 'walkie talkie' glint alluringly from The City, whilst Grenfell remains shrouded in its funereal sheath of scaffold wrap.

Thoughts turn forward to the journey ahead and preconceptions and notions of the North. I was born in the North, Leeds, but like others whose parents moved south for opportunity, never fully returned other than for trips to visit grandparents, Leeds United's Elland Road and regular holidays in Scarborough.

What is the North? Midlands to the south, Scottish Borders to the north. This vast area comprises much of England's national parkland, but also great swathes of urbanisation arising from the Industrial Revolution and resultant economies based on large-scale industry and the mechanised manufacturing of the factory system. At the 2011 census, the conurbations of South Yorkshire and West Yorkshire, Greater Manchester, Merseyside, Tyneside, Wearside and Teeside had a combined population of 9.5 million and Northern England as a whole 14.9 million.

These are the facts, but does the North of England have particular cultural codes and aesthetics that set it apart? Clearly the individual regions of the North have had their own cultural identities going back centuries, but with the industrialisation of the nineteenth and twentieth centuries came

Trinity Square, Gateshead
Designed by Rodney Gordon
for the Owen Luder Partnership
Built 1962–69, demolished 2010

a more homogenised version of the Northerner, later reinforced by the growth of mass media. Stereotypical cultural traits such as 'plain-speaking' and 'grit' combine with representational items of clothing – flat-caps and casual sportswear – to create a convenient set of characteristics and style with which to identify northernness. The South is implicit in forming a collective delusion about the qualities that define and represent this northernness: miners, pits, back-to-backs, heavy industry, soot, rugby league, slagheaps, racing pigeons, the Orgreave battle during the 1980s' miners strike and the cultural phenomenon of Madchester.

Of course, many of these signifiers are now long gone, but the tropes persist. All cities are products of the myths that inhabit their materiality; literature, films, received wisdom and false consciousness inform and impinge upon our perceptions. Thus Newcastle upon Tyne and Gateshead will forever be associated with the *Get Carter* car park. *Get Carter* is a tough seventies northern film-noir in which Michael Caine, playing the most unbelievable Geordie ever appointed by a casting agent, tosses a large man who's in bad shape off the roof of Trinity Square car park. The Trinity Square multi-storey car park and shopping complex was a masterpiece of gothic Brutalism designed by the great Rodney Gordon for the Owen Luder Partnership. The car park was tragically demolished in 2010.

Forton Services, Lancaster
Designed by Bill Galloway and
Ray Anderson of TP Bennett and Son
Built 1964–65, listed grade II, P.167

Road signs direct me up the country, the white arrow sitting emphatically on the rich blue of the Pantone 300 ground. The clear lettering defined by modernist ambition informs me that I am heading to the North; 'The NORTH' as signed by Jock Kinneir and Margaret Calvert, who, in undertaking the design of a new signage system for the roads, embarked upon one of the most ambitious information design projects ever to happen in Britain. Between 1957 and 1967 they created a rigorous system of carefully coordinated lettering, colours and shapes. The two new typefaces were called 'Transport' and 'Motorway', and since my early years I have always been thrilled by the clarity with which the signs tell me I am heading in the right direction when I return to the North. As Margaret Calvert put it: 'You were driving towards the absolute essence. How could we reduce the appearance to make the maximum sense?' The new typeface, a refinement of sans serif Akzidenz-Grotesk, was tested on the Preston bypass (now part of the M6) on which traffic speeds under the pedestrian bridge of the remarkable Forton Services. Motorists are no longer able to indulge in fine dining in the air-traffic-control-themed

Pennine Tower as it was closed to the public in 1989, but in its day, TP Bennett and Son's 20-metre-high tower of 1964–65 provided not only a cantilevered restaurant from which to survey the countryside but also a 'luxury sun deck'. The Beatles were apparently one of its first customers, but present-day fare is less glamorous and now we have to be satisfied with Burger King.

Coming off the motorway at Junction 32, it's time to take a look at one of the early boomtowns of the new industrial North. Preston, previously a market town and known in the eighteenth century as 'Proud Preston', underwent rapid population and economic growth as new technologies such as Richard Arkwright's spinning frame powered the massive textile factories. Alongside the newfound prosperity of the town came degrees of Enlightenment that would result in the building of such edifices of self-improvement as James Hibbert's neo-classical Harris Museum. Hibbert's defining qualities for the Harris were 'simplicity, symmetry of plan, truthfulness of expression and refinement of detail'. One of the inscriptions carved on the external walls of the building, taken from the meditations of Marcus Aurelius, promises: 'The mental riches you may here acquire abide with you always.'

The counterbalance to the shafts of liberal light that Enlightened thought cast was the grinding poverty and oppression of the new working class. Having visited Preston, Karl Marx, in the *New-York Daily Tribune* in 1854, declared: 'The eyes of the working classes are now fully opened: they begin to cry: "Our St. Petersburg is at Preston!"'

Traditions of trade unionism and collectivism were strong in Preston and so the socialist proposition behind Building Design Partnership, now better known as BDP, although radical, was perhaps unsurprising. George Grenfell-Baines, who took the Bauhaus integrated and interdisciplinary model as his inspiration, formed Building Design Partnership in Preston in 1961. The early collective nature of BDP emphasised the collaborative rather than the individual and was the end result of a process of profit sharing and multidisciplinary working begun by Grenfell-Baines in 1941. In *BDP Continuous Collective* of 2011, GG (as Grenfell-Baines was affectionately known) is quoted: 'One great discovery was of Walter Gropius and his bringing together of artists, sculptors, industrial designers, photographers, and architects in an attempt to create a unity of arts and technology . . . What had only been sensed darkly became brilliantly clear. Why not do this with the building industry and the professions? Group practices of all the disciplines! Technology and art linking together in fruitful dialectic relationships!'

Preston bus station is now rightly considered a Brutalist masterpiece and was granted grade II listed building status

Preston Central Bus Station and Car Park
Designed by Keith Ingham and Charles Wilson of Building Design Partnership
Built 1968–69, listed grade II, P.169

in 2013. Designed by Keith Ingham and Charles Wilson of Building Design Partnership, the bus station was built between 1968 and 1969. With its sweeping, shell-edged balcony edges and dynamically helical vehicle ramps, this megastructure has a truly sculptural presence and strength that sits comfortably alongside the tough civic buildings of Preston's Victorian pomp. Up until 2012 the bus station was threatened with demolition; one early proposal was to replace it with a shopping centre, for which, ironically, the architects were to have been BDP.

Thankfully the bus station did remain and has been sympathetically renovated and reorganised, by John Puttick Associates and Cassidy + Ashton, whilst Preston Council has also reorganised their priorities regarding shopping centres by implementing the 'Preston Model', which focuses on principles of localism and community wealth building.

Preston's positive approach points away from the North of recent years, where fashionable architects and urban-visionaries such as Will Alsop provide masterplans for elevating rundown northern pit-towns into bustling neo-Tuscan hill towns, as in the Barnsley plan of 2002. One would hope that if the masterplan had been adopted, rather than being ditched as too expensive, Barnsley's reinvention might have fared somewhat better than Manchester's more recent 'Chips' building of 2009. Alsop's residential block was intended to represent 'three fat chips stacked on top of each other', a giant Claes-Oldenburg-style sculpture that would not have survived an encounter with a deep fat fryer as it turns out that, on recent inspection, post-Grenfell, the panels cladding the 'chips' were labelled as being 'non-fire retardant'. Unfortunately, this seems to be symptomatic of many new developments that are erasing the post-war legacy of the sixties and seventies, much of which was strong and characterful architecture resonating with architect, critic and historian Kenneth Frampton's thoughts on Critical Regionalism: an architecture that resists the placelessness and loss of identity of International Modernism, and seeks a specific architectural response to regional identities, landscape and culture whilst still remaining determinedly modern.

Dunelm House, Durham
Designed by Michael Powers and Richard Raines of Architects Co-Partnership
Built 1966, P.081

Dunelm House's craggy form grows up the steep gorge from the edge of the River Wear. Designed by Architects Co-Partnership, the student union of the University of Durham sits alongside the elegant span of Kingsgate Bridge, designed by Ove Arup, which links town and gown. The building is a series of stratified decks and block-concrete forms pierced with irregular windows and overlaid mullions ramping down the precipitous gorge. Interlinking forms resemble a giant abstracted geological outcrop; the use of topography, massing and masonry and its relation to the vertical thrust of Durham's breath-taking cathedral viewed across Arup's bridge create an ensemble of innovative, challenging and beautiful forms that sit comfortably with ideas of critical regionalism. Regrettably, the university doesn't hold Dunelm House in much esteem and would prefer to rid the gorge of this remarkable sculptural form, deeming it 'unfit' for purpose.

A great deal of the post-war architecture of the North can be characterised as uncompromising, and it is worth considering the precedents set by the Victorians at the height of their prosperity. Cuthbert Brodrick's Leeds Town Hall was built from 1853 and opened by Queen Victoria in 1858. With its tower standing at 68.6 metres, it was the tallest building in Leeds until 1966. It defines northern civic bombast and was the go-to template and inspiration for any number of civic copyists, both national and international, from Bolton Town Hall to Philadelphia City Hall. Its classical certitude, rationality and order are embodied in the serried ranks of the giant Corinthian order of columns supporting the deeply recessed portico sitting atop a heavily rusticated and monstrous base of millstone grit. If the main building was not enough of a showpiece to establish Leeds as the pre-eminent city of the North, it was decided that, at an additional cost of £5,500, a clock tower was needed. The tower is composed of a deep plinth with rusticated panels and a square colonnade supporting the clock dials and a huge concave, lead-clad dome. Frivolity is not to be entertained – it is stern, harsh, sullen and brutal. Monumental art is assuredly glowering down at us, and is captured strikingly on the record sleeve of Gang of Four's 1980 single 'Outside the Trains Don't Run on Time': discordant, dangerous, seditious funk chiming perfectly with the untrammelled aggression of the baroque leviathan.

Sunderland Civic Centre
Designed by John Bonnington of Sir Basil Spence, Bonnington and Collins
Built 1965, PP.120–121

The post-war period was also assuredly civic in its architectural output, with many northern cities asserting pride through a new civic centre or extended town hall. Sunderland Civic Centre, designed in 1965 by the architectural practice of Sir Basil Spence, Bonnington and Collins, with John S Bonnington as the lead architect, is a terraced, ramped and stepped arrangement in brindled brick, concrete and red brick tiles. The low informal group was planned to sit into the sloping site and designed as two linked hexagonal blocks with another half hexagon acting as an administration building. The hexagons wrap around spacious planted courtyards, the ramped terracing running through as the centre steps up the slope from the battered rampart-like walls below, giving the impression of entering an artfully designed fortress. The tough-looking brindle brick expanses of wall alternate with continuous strip windows that extend around all sides and levels of the centre – a watchful command centre surveying the town.

Once seen as a sign of status and the town's desire for self-promotion, Sunderland Civic Centre was glowingly reviewed: 'A recognizable addition to the scene of the industrial and maritime character and history of Sunderland ... this unusual collection of hexagons truly graces the eminence on which it stands' (HAN Brockman, *Financial Times*, 6 November 1970). The building was also the recipient of a Royal Institute of British Architects Gold Medal and a Civic Trust Award. However, current thinking in austerity-riven times is that the centre is too expensive to run and council relocation and demolition is the answer.

Carlisle Civic Centre
Designed by Charles B Pearson and Partners
Built 1964, P.166

By contrast, Carlisle's Civic Centre is an intriguing podium and tower bookended by the hexagonal rotunda of the council chamber. In appearance the rotunda could have been a small tower lifted from the Smithsons' Economist Buildings in London. The council offices housed within the tower are almost Miesian in intention but contained within a reinforced concrete frame reminiscent of a Sol LeWitt minimalist cuboid sculpture. Designed by Charles B Pearson, Son and Partners and completed in 1965, this monochromatic Rubik's cube is an unusual and exciting architectural arrangement to be found within a traditional border town with a medieval castle and city walls. Sadly, in 2015, Storm Desmond left the ground floor of the centre under water; the council estimates it would cost £144,000 to refurbish and, as such, the best and most cost-effective restoration strategy is to demolish the rotunda and replace it with a car park ...

There is an emerging theme of hard-pressed councils closing or reducing the scale of their once prestigious and ambitious civic offices. In Wigan, photographing the former civic centre, which is now closed down, and composing the picture, I am momentarily lost in thought and roused from it by yobbish jeering. Two inebriated young men have interposed themselves between the camera and the civic centre, demanding that I take their picture. I readily agree – after all, what have I got to lose? Placation seems to be the best form of defence. Inevitably, once my eye is to the camera, the V-signs are flicked, accompanied by an alarming display of gurning. The shutter clicks, mission accomplished, they then depart cheerfully. As I watch them chunter off I wonder what they imagine is to happen to this momentary 1/125 record of their drunken intervention. It's not as though they asked me for a copy.

This is a sub-theme – not all drunken, I hasten to add – of my northern excursions: a desire on the part of a number of individuals to be framed and captured against a backdrop of northern modernism, a conscious claiming of the film plane, populating my purposefully uninhabited modernist landscape, demanding to be present within it. An image of Kevin Cummins' 1979 photograph of Joy Division set on the bleak, minimalist, receding perspective of a pedestrian bridge comes to mind. Perhaps this is what my drunken interventionists helpfully had in mind, sensing that my composition needed people to complete it. Or maybe they were just trying to fuck with my picture.

Wigan Civic Centre
Designed by Percy Thomas Partnership
Built 1970, P.176

Musicians are often posed against architectural backdrops for their publicity shots, and architecture has been used to great effect on record covers. From the graphically rendered New York tenements of Led Zeppelin's *Physical Graffiti* to Rut Blees Luxemburg's other-worldly, sodium-lit night shot of a 1960s tower block adorning The Streets' *Original Pirate Material*, the architectural cover not only alludes to the concerns of the record therein (Luxemburg says of the album: 'The sentiment of the lyrics to articulate this other experience of living in the city, really chimes with my work. It's what I was trying to express visually – these places are hothouses of creativity') but it can also speak of the relation between music and architecture. Terms such as rhythm, texture, harmony, proportion, dynamics and articulation are as applicable to both music and architecture. Sound patterns and beats become the repetition of orders both regular and irregular in the built form. The regimented order of the Corinthian columns marching across the Gang of Four's aforementioned record sleeve suggests both the structural nature of civic power but also the rhythmic, staccato, austere sound etched into the vinyl.

Outside the Trains Don't Run on Time, Gang of Four, 1980

The Gang of Four was formed in the city of Leeds; the image of Leeds Town Hall on the sleeve was no coincidence. They were graduates of the progressive and radical Fine Art department of the University of Leeds, where Guy Debord's *The Society of the Spectacle*, analysing the alienating effects of mass media and entertainment, was consumed within the radical precincts of the Leeds University Campus Extension. The Leeds Development Plan of 1960 by architects Chamberlin, Powell and Bon was a landmark in the development of the New Universities, the first plan to consider the university environment holistically. Structured around the concept of the 'ten-minute university'

Campus Expansion, University of Leeds
Designed by Chamberlin, Powell and Bon
Built 1963–78, PP.047–048

– the central consideration that taking longer than ten minutes to walk from any point to point was a waste of time – resulted in the spectacular rationalist megastructure of walkways and buildings. The clean, sweeping lines, repeated structural patterns and ribbon glazing that constitute the campus extension of the sixties and seventies step down the site from north to south maintaining a continuous roof line and levels; a device that was also used at Park Hill in Sheffield.

The remarkable sight and siting of Sheffield's Park Hill Estate still holds its power 59 years after it was opened. Begun in 1957 the housing estate, designed by Jack Lynn and Ivor Smith under JL Womersley of Sheffield Corporation City Architect's Department, presents a vast image, a continuous wall that folds around the steep, blunted hill that rises up from the railway cut below. The form that unwraps creates a single unified and resolute megastructure that can be seen in long-view from around the city. The regularity of the structural frame and the dwellings contained within were intended to provide consistency from one end of the site to the other and, whilst the roofline remains constant, the change in ground level means that the building steps from four storeys to fourteen. This 'unity of place' is now being challenged by the differing approaches being made by Urban Splash on their staged redevelopment of Park Hill, and we have moved from the acid pop colours of Hawkins\Brown and Studio Egret West to a 'light touch', neutral approach by architects Mikhail Riches. Nonetheless, it is still possible to see the clearness of vision that Reyner Banham recognised in his review in *Architectural Review* in December 1961: 'Park Hill seems to represent one of those rare occasions when the intention to create a certain kind of architecture happens to encounter a programme and a site that can hardly be dealt with in any other way, and the result has the clarity that only arises when ... aesthetic programme and functional opportunity meet and are instantly fused. But what Park Hill abundantly demonstrates is that there are other kinds of architectural clarity besides the Classical.'

Park Hill, Sheffield
Designed by Jack Lynn, Ivor Smith and Frederick Nicklin of Sheffield City Architects' Department (under John Lewis Womersley)
Built 1958–61, listed grade II*, P.069

The North of England figured prominently in the 1960s, and Harold Wilson's emphasis on the 'white heat of technology' provided a slogan of scientific modernity to add to the spectacular ambition of the North's post-war rebuilding. Wilson later reflected that his hope was to 'replace the cloth cap [with] the white laboratory coat as the symbol of British labour'. The counterpoint to this

Grotesque (After the Gramme), The Fall, 1980. Cover Illustration by Suzanne Smith

was the similarly spectacular upsurge in popular culture, particularly in music, with bands such as the Beatles and the Animals rising to international prominence. As disillusionment and antipathy to this 'pop' and 'rock' grew through the late 1970s, perhaps reflecting the decay and dereliction that had been allowed to take root in schemes such as the Hulme Crescents in Manchester, a seditious counterculture grew to replace the newly perceived irrelevance of the rock supergroups.

'The N.W.R.A.' (or North Will Rise Again) is a song from the album *Grotesque (After the Gramme)* released in 1980 by Manchester band the Fall. In it, Mark E Smith talks in a characteristically discursive, rambling and cut-up form about vague plots to restore the North to something approximating its former eminence, possibly alluding to the one-time economic dominance of its industrial heyday. Factory chimneys once adorned the cityscapes like a new and grotesque plantation spewing forth soot and filth rather than buds and sap; now it is: 'The estates [that] stick up like stacks ... The North had rose again. But it would turn out wrong.' In Smith's vision the North had come to stand for everything suppressed by the metropolitan proprieties of good taste, the esoteric and the aesthetic, and would regain its identity through an unspecified uprising wherein:

The streets of Soho did reverberate
With drunken Highland men
Revenge for Culloden dead.

It seems unlikely, though, that Smith, however psychic, would have conceived that the agency by which the North would supposedly regain its pre-eminence would be George Osborne.

Thirty-four years after the release of *Grotesque*, in a keynote speech, then-Conservative Chancellor George Osborne's stated desire was to create a 'Northern Powerhouse'. According to the Northern Powerhouse Strategy, published by HM Treasury in November 2016, its aims were to 'address key barriers to productivity in the region'. The government would also 'invest in transport infrastructure to improve connections between and within the North's towns, cities and counties; work with local areas to raise education and skills levels across the North; ensure the North is an excellent place to start and grow a business; and ensure the Northern Powerhouse is recognised worldwide as an excellent opportunity for trade and investment'.

Exploring the transport infrastructure of the Northern Powerhouse by driving across the Pennines on the M62, Britain's highest motorway, in lashing rain and gale-force winds, doesn't

High Point, Bradford
John Tempest for John Brunton Partnership
1972, P.021

seem like a wise decision. Juggernauts send out huge gouts of spray as they churn their way up to the summit and descend past the vaguely absurd Stott Hall Farm – due to a geological fault, the eastbound and westbound carriageways of the M62 diverge at this point and then merge again, leaving the farm trapped on a 15-acre agricultural island. *Concrete Island* by JG Ballard comes to mind: after a motor accident, architect Robert Maitland is left stranded in a large area of derelict land created by several intersecting motorways. This could be the everyday-story-of-country-folk version and I need to be careful not to aquaplane through the crash barrier and spend the rest of my life living on sheep carcasses and flossing my teeth with bailing twine. I'm travelling to Bradford, and it always seems to rain when I go to Bradford, but this is more than rain – it is a life-threatening biblical deluge.

Having survived the journey I park, thankful that the rain has eased a bit. I can photograph in most weather and enjoy the contrasting effects that differing light conditions bring to a subject. But rain isn't good: great fat blobs on the lens distort and blur the architectural elevation committed to the memory card. It's only later, once the image processing begins, that the offending blob is noticed and the cursing begins. No, rain is decidedly not good.

It might be the third time I have attempted to photograph High Point, which began life as Bradford Permanent Building Society headquarters. Designed by John Tempest of Bradford-based practice John Brunton and Partners and built in 1972, High Point became the Yorkshire Building Society in 1983. High Point rears up over the city, a gigantic eight-storey slab of corrugated concrete punctuated by golden-red reflective glass slit windows. Like a resolute latter-day castle's keep, it is Bradford's standout Brutalist building and its visual narrative is entirely consistent with the concept of safeguarding savings. Some sunlight would be good – it would transmute the ribbed concrete forms into something approaching a giant Georges Vantongerloo sculpture; predictably, though, I wait out the rain until it becomes mere drizzle and accept that, for me, High Point will always be synonymous with heavy, rain-filled skies and dark, weather-stained concrete, but still splendid nonetheless.

Strangely, given the repetitiveness of Osborne's much-vaunted claims, and subsequent bleated promises of 'levelling up' by Boris Johnson, it was a one-time Trotskyist painter and decorator and subsequent Labour leader of Newcastle Council who, several decades earlier, had had the visionary foresight to promote the North as having the potential to be a huge autonomous regional power. As council leader from 1960–65,

Byker Estate, Newcastle upon Tyne
Designed by Ralph Erskine and Vernon Gracie
Built 1969–82, P.101

T Dan Smith's vision would lead to the re-imagining of Newcastle as 'The Brasilia of the North'. This aspiration had been kick-started with the demolition of the slums of Scotswood and the implementation of an ambitious housing programme that would culminate in the Byker Estate replacing a great swathe of unfit and derelict terraced housing. Ralph Erskine's visionary design for the new housing, built between 1969 and 1982 and known locally as the Byker Wall, emerged from community engagement. The architects opened an office on-site, somewhat bizarrely (maybe as a nod to the last rites of the decaying fabric of Byker) in an old funeral parlour, and Vernon Gracie, the site architect, lived in a flat above. This was to foster good communication and understanding with residents, as the estate was being built while the existing housing was demolished. The consultative process resulted in the bright colours, balconies, courtyards and play areas of the scheme. The most distinctive element of the estate is the wall, designed to buffer traffic sound and wind from the housing behind it. The wall is sheer but mitigated by abstract patterning in the brickwork and the punctuation of tiny windows and colourful air vents. On the other side of the wall, however, a joyous display of coloured wooden balconies, corrugated roofs, and multiple walkways look out onto extensive views and the jumble of low-rise housing and open spaces below. Widely regarded as a success both architecturally and by the residents, the Byker Estate should be regarded as a model for public housing to be developed further; although there should be misgivings that despite the efforts at public engagement, only 20 per cent of local residents of Byker were actually rehoused on the estate.

As well as housing, Smith's achievements in other areas were significant. The heavily polluted Tyne was cleaned under his direction. Newcastle airport was expanded to become an international airport by 1967. International architects and artists, including Le Corbusier and Picasso, were invited to work in the city, and an advisory committee for the new Newcastle comprised Basil Spence, Robert Matthew and Arne Jacobsen. Northern Arts had been founded. The Tyneside Metro was on its way, Newcastle University had established itself as an independent entity and the polytechnic had been founded and sited in a central precinct. Traffic congestion had been much diminished by a new motorway network and the fine George Kenyon-designed civic centre had been built.

In a documentary from 1970, a big and tall, florid-faced, smartly suited man known as 'Mr Newcastle', 'The Voice of the North' and, more unkindly, 'The Tyne Mouth', sits at the top of Claremont Tower at the University of Newcastle. The view takes in the newly completed Scandinavian-influenced civic centre. T Dan Smith eloquently engages with the camera: 'We should create in the northern region for the first time, in my lifetime, a region which would be relevant to tomorrow rather than always running after this illusion of prosperity.' The documentary was one in a series of British government-sponsored TV programmes called *The Pacemakers* and profiled innovative and maverick contributors to British life. By now, Smith was the chairman of the Northern Economic Planning Council and his remit was to plan and implement a successful future for the North. As a member of a commission on local government he promoted a scheme to break England down into five provinces with wide-ranging autonomy. In Smith's 1970 autobiography he reflects on his vision of a truly internationalist North in which counties were 'cut down to size and parochial jealousies ironed out'. The North would have had Manchester as its capital and a population of 17,000,000 people.

Tragically, T Dan Smith was to become enmeshed in a huge corruption scandal involving property developers, planners, councillors, builders, police chiefs, politicians and freemasons. Most crucially, though, his links to the corrupt architect John Poulson were to result in his standing trial for bribery of officials for building contracts. According to his own testimony, Smith was brought low by stress, heart disease and a diet of 'Carlsberg Special Brew and Valium'. He was unable to adequately defend himself and was sentenced to six years in jail, emerging in 1977 a broken man. Perhaps fittingly, he spent his last years campaigning for penal reform with the Howard League whilst living in his fourteenth-floor tower block flat at Cruddas Park, one of the developments that replaced the slum housing of Scotswood Road all those years before. He died in 1993.

Dan Smith from the documentary series *The Pacemakers*, 1970

It is still possible, however, to see the remnants of T Dan Smith's civic vision, and his achievements shouldn't be overlooked. It is telling that the ambitions of Osborne's Northern Powerhouse manifesto can not hold a light to Smith's all-encompassing vision for housing, education, industry, communications, culture and internationalism in a democratic, socially engaged and autonomous North. It is also telling that Smith and other civic leaders, as well as dreaming, also got things done: looking at the small list of achievements credited to the Northern Powerhouse since it was formed in 2015, it pales into insignificance in comparison to the North of the post-war years and the determination of its civic convictions and drive to create a proud and better society for all. The buildings in *Brutal North* are testimony to the scale of that ambition.

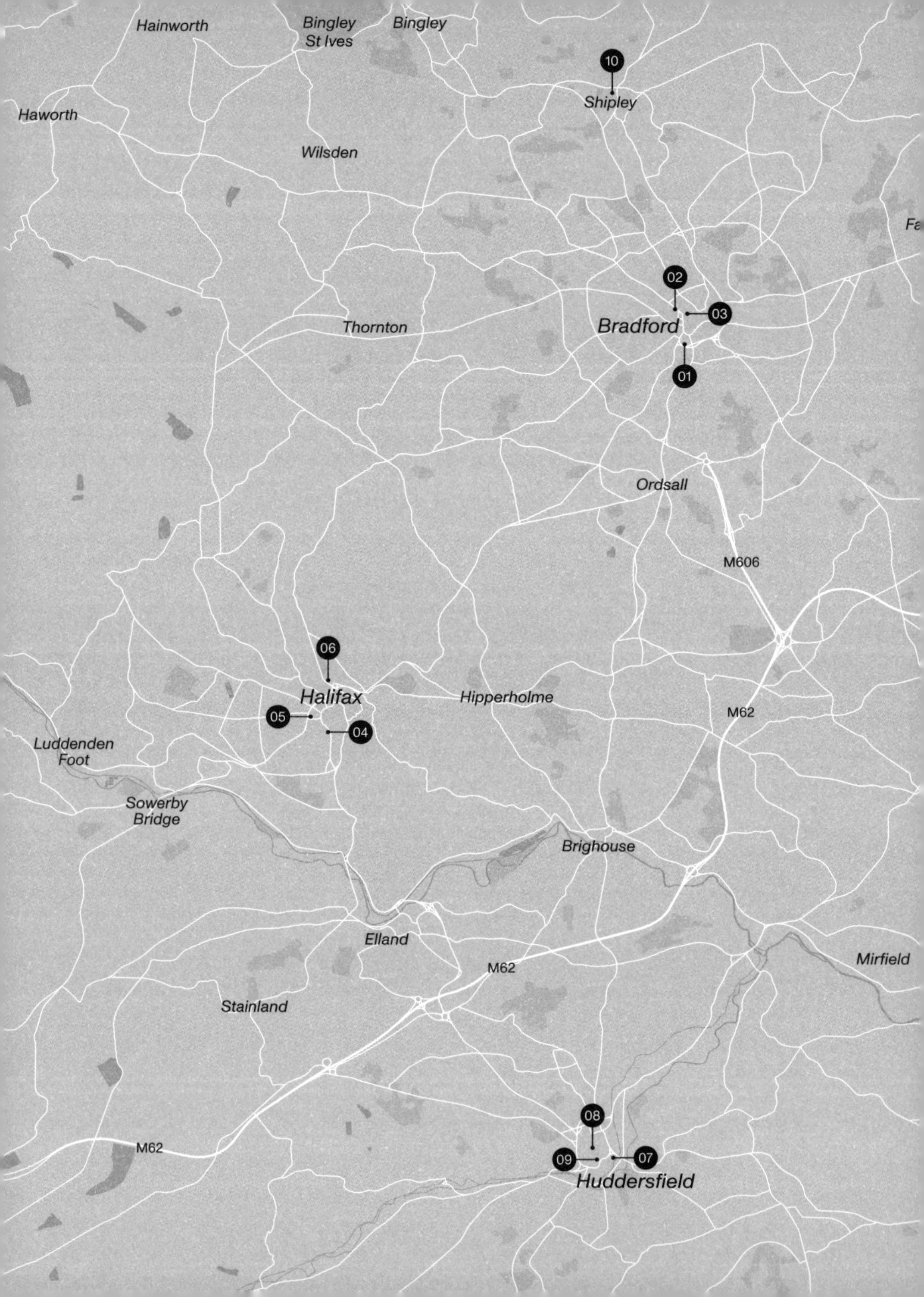
Hainworth
Bingley St Ives
Bingley
10
Shipley
Haworth
Wilsden
02
03
Thornton
Bradford
01
Ordsall
M606
06
Halifax
Hipperholme
05
04
M62
Luddenden Foot
Sowerby Bridge
Brighouse
Elland
M62
Mirfield
Stainland
08
09
07
M62
Huddersfield

Yorkshire & Humberside

Bradford & Huddersfield

Bradford, Central Telephone Exchange, 1976

Bradford, High Point, 1972

Bradford, Kirkgate Centre, 1974

Halifax Building, 1968–74

← Halifax, Elim Pentecostal Church, 1972

↑ Halifax, Haley Court, 1968

Huddersfield, Central Services Building, 1973–77

Huddersfield, Midland Bank, 1970

Huddersfield, Queensgate Market, 1968–70

Shipley Market, 1957–60

Bentley
Dunswell
Cottingham Parks
Golf & Leisure Club
05
Bransholm
Cottingham
University
of Hull
07
03
02
08
Hull
Willerby
04
Anlaby
06
Hessle
01
River Humber
Humber Bridge
Barrow Haven

Yorkshire & Humberside

Hull & Humber

01 Hessle, Humber Bridge
02 Hull, Brynmor Jones Library
03 Hull, Gulbenkian Centre
04 Hull, Kingston House
05 Hull, The Lawns
06 Hull, Tidal Surge Barrier
07 Hull, University Sports Centre
08 Hull, Wilberforce Building

Public Access
Prohibited

← Hessle, Humber Bridge, 1973–81

↑ Hull, Brynmor Jones Library, 1956–69

Hull, Gulbenkian Centre, 1967–69

Hull, Kingston House, 1965–67

Hull, The Lawns, 1963–68

Hull, Tidal Surge Barrier, 1977–80

Hull, University Sports Centre, 1963–65

Hull, Wilberforce Building, 1968–70

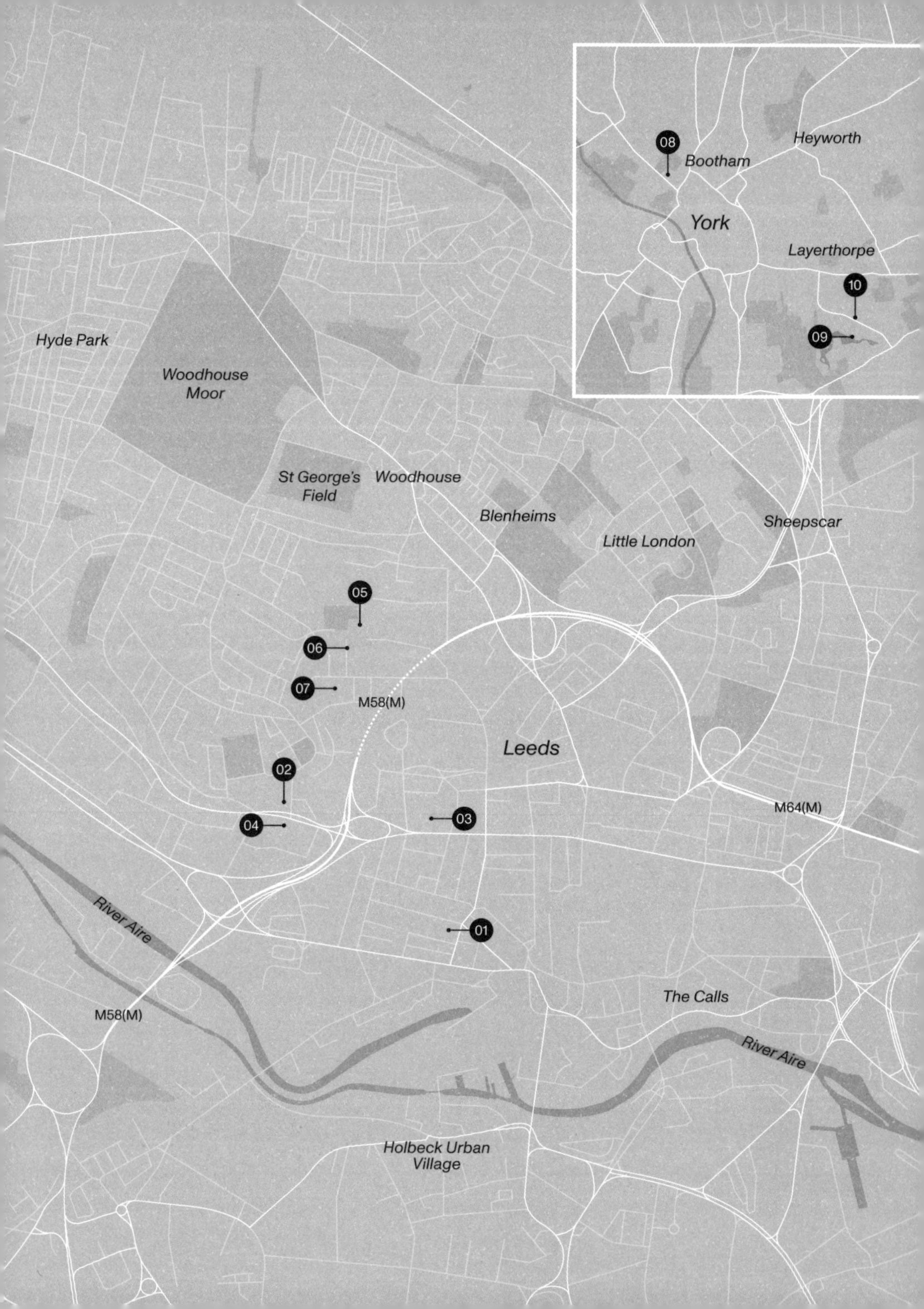
08
Bootham
Heyworth
York
Layerthorpe
10
09
Hyde Park
Woodhouse Moor
St George's Field
Woodhouse
Blenheims
Little London
Sheepscar
05
06
07
M58(M)
Leeds
02
04
03
M64(M)
River Aire
01
The Calls
M58(M)
River Aire
Holbeck Urban Village

Yorkshire & Humberside

Leeds & York

01 Leeds, Bank House
02 Leeds City College University Centre
03 Leeds, Combined Court Centre
04 Leeds, Marlborough Towers
05 Leeds, Roger Stevens Building
06 Leeds, Campus Expansion
07 Leeds, Worsley Building
08 York, Assembly Hall, Bootham School
09 York, Central Hall
10 York, JB Morrell Library

Leeds, Bank House, 1969–71

Leeds City College University Centre, 1970s

Leeds, Combined Court Centre, 1982

↑ Leeds, Marlborough Towers, 1963–66

→ Leeds, Roger Stevens Building, 1968–71

← Leeds, Campus Expansion, 1963–78

↑ Leeds, Worsley Building, 1976–79

York, Assembly Hall, Bootham School, 1965–66

↑ York, Central Hall, 1966–68

→ York, JB Morrell Library, 1965–66

UNIVERSITY LIBRARY

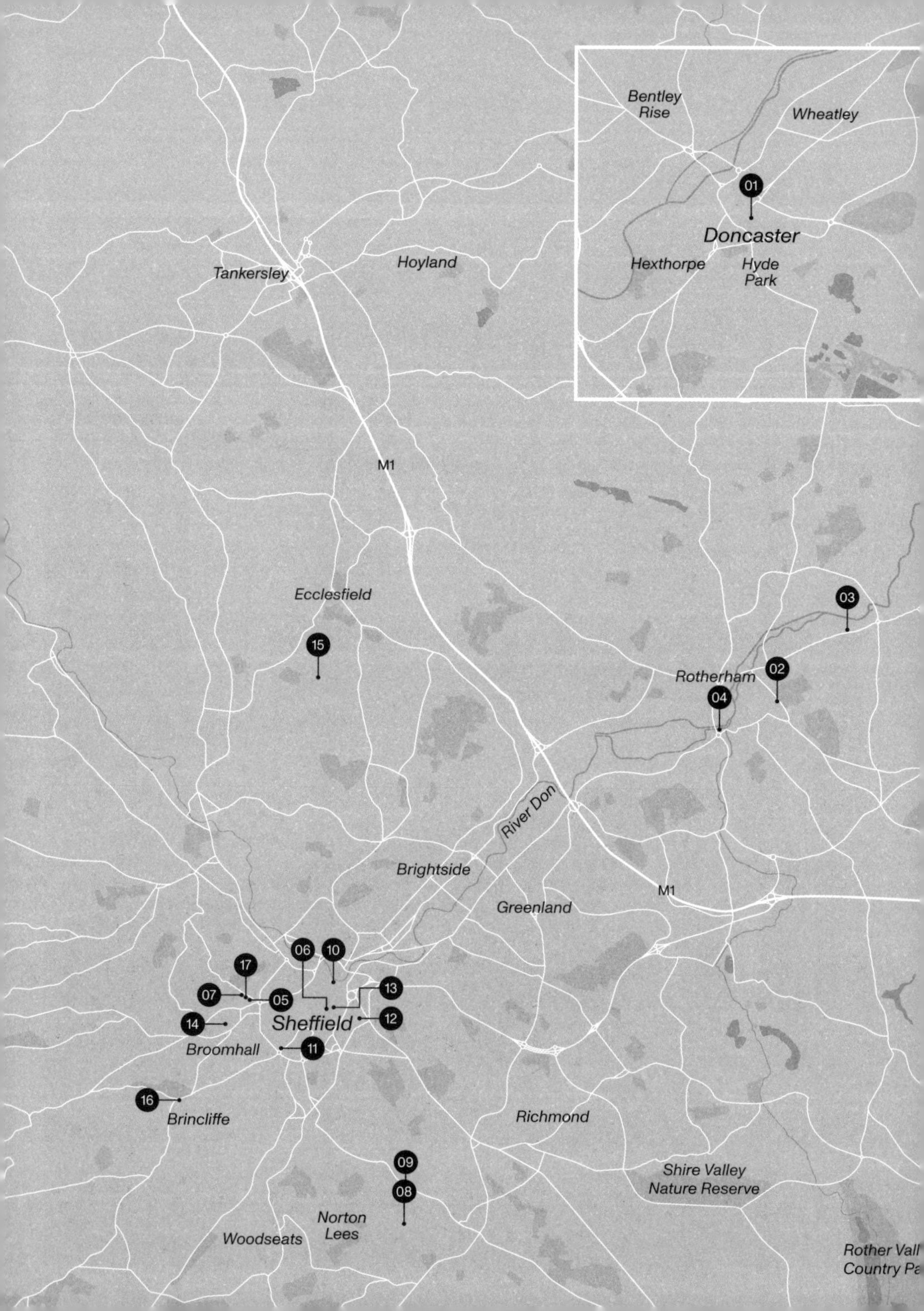
Bentley Rise
Wheatley
01
Doncaster
Hexthorpe
Hyde Park
Tankersley
Hoyland
M1
Ecclesfield
03
15
02
Rotherham
04
River Don
Brightside
M1
Greenland
06
10
17
13
07
05
14
Sheffield
12
Broomhall
11
16
Brincliffe
Richmond
09
08
Shire Valley Nature Reserve
Norton Lees
Woodseats

Yorkshire & Humberside

Doncaster, Rotherham, Sheffield

01 Doncaster Magistrates' Court and Police Station
02 Rotherham, Beeversleigh Flats
03 Rotherham, Fire Training Centre
04 Rotherham, Marsh Street Pumping Station
05 Sheffield, Arts Tower
06 Sheffield, Crucible Theatre
07 Sheffield, Department of Geography
08 Sheffield, Gleadless Valley Estate
09 Sheffield, Holy Cross Church
10 Sheffield Magistrates' Court
11 Sheffield, Moore Street Electricity Substation
12 Sheffield, Park Hill
13 Sheffield, Pond Street Entertainment Complex
14 Sheffield, Royal Hallamshire Hospital
15 Sheffield, St Paul's Church
16 Sheffield, Trinity United Reformed Church
17 Sheffield, Western Bank Library

Doncaster Magistrates' Court and Police Station, 1969

↑ Rotherham, Beeversleigh Flats, 1970–71

→ Rotherham, Fire Training Centre, date unknown

← Rotherham, Marsh Street Pumping Station, date unknown ↑ Sheffield, Arts Tower, 1962–65

Sheffield, Crucible Theatre, 1969–71

Sheffield, Department of Geography, 1970–71

Sheffield, Gleadless Valley Estate, 1955–62

← Sheffield, Holy Cross Church, 1964–65

↑ Sheffield Magistrates' Court, 1978

Sheffield, Moore Street Electricity Substation, 1968

Sheffield, Park Hill, 1958–61

Sheffield, Pond Street Entertainment Complex, 1965

Sheffield, Royal Hallamshire Hospital, 1968–78

Sheffield, St Paul's Church, 1958–59

↑ Sheffield, Trinity United Reformed Church, 1970–71

→ Sheffield, Western Bank Library, 1959

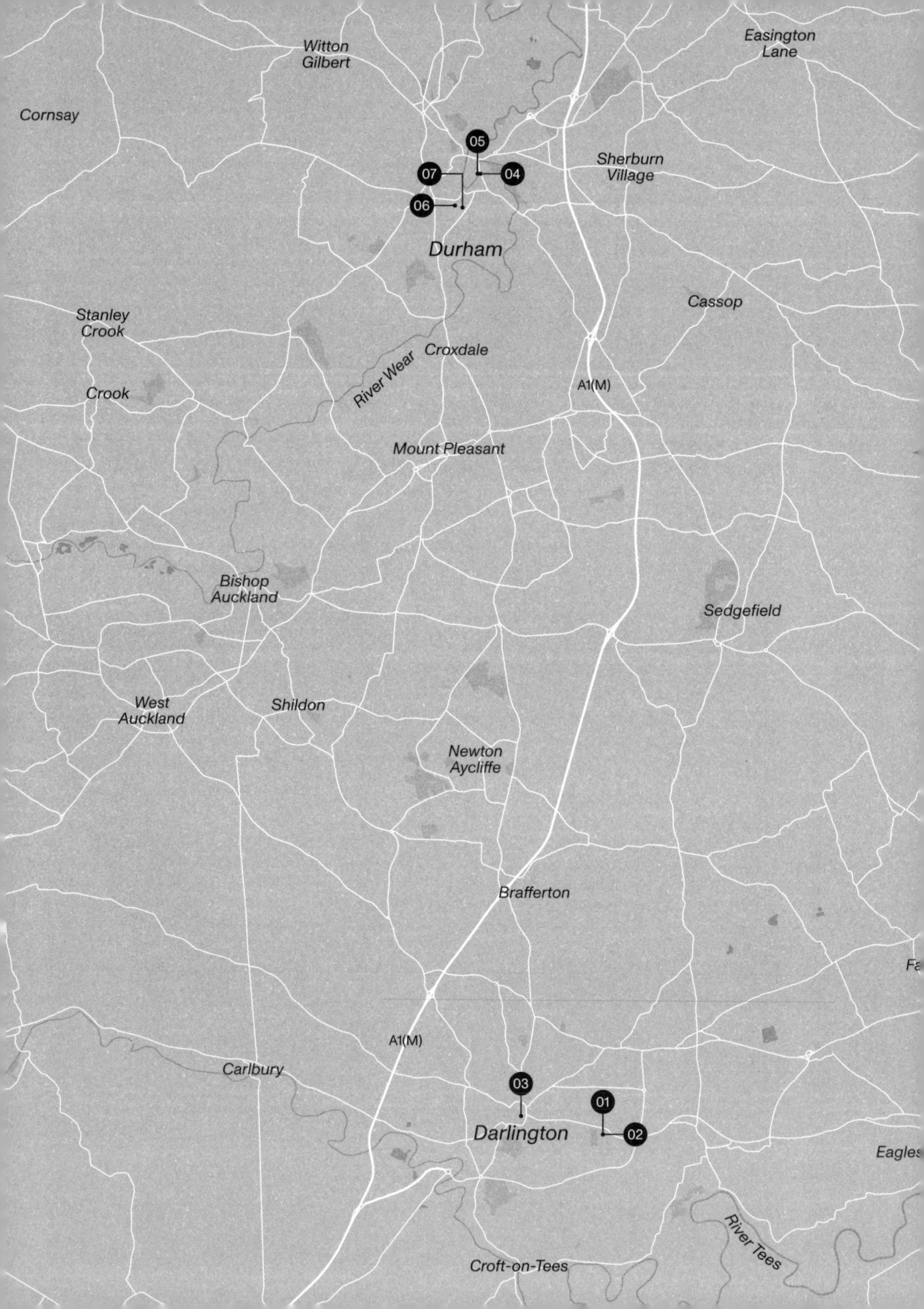
Witton Gilbert
Easington Lane
Cornsay
05
07
04
Sherburn Village
06
Durham
Stanley Crook
Cassop
Croxdale
River Wear
Crook
A1(M)
Mount Pleasant
Bishop Auckland
Sedgefield
West Auckland
Shildon
Newton Aycliffe
Brafferton
A1(M)
Carlbury
03
01
Darlington
02
River Tees
Croft-on-Tees

North East

Darlington & Durham

Darlington, Cummins Manufacturing Facility, 1963–64

Darlington, Cummins Engine Factory, 1964–65

Darlington Town Hall, 1967–70

Durham, Dunelm House, 1964–66

Durham, Kingsgate Bridge, 1963

↑ Durham, Trevelyan College, 1965–67

→ Durham, St Aidan's College, 1964

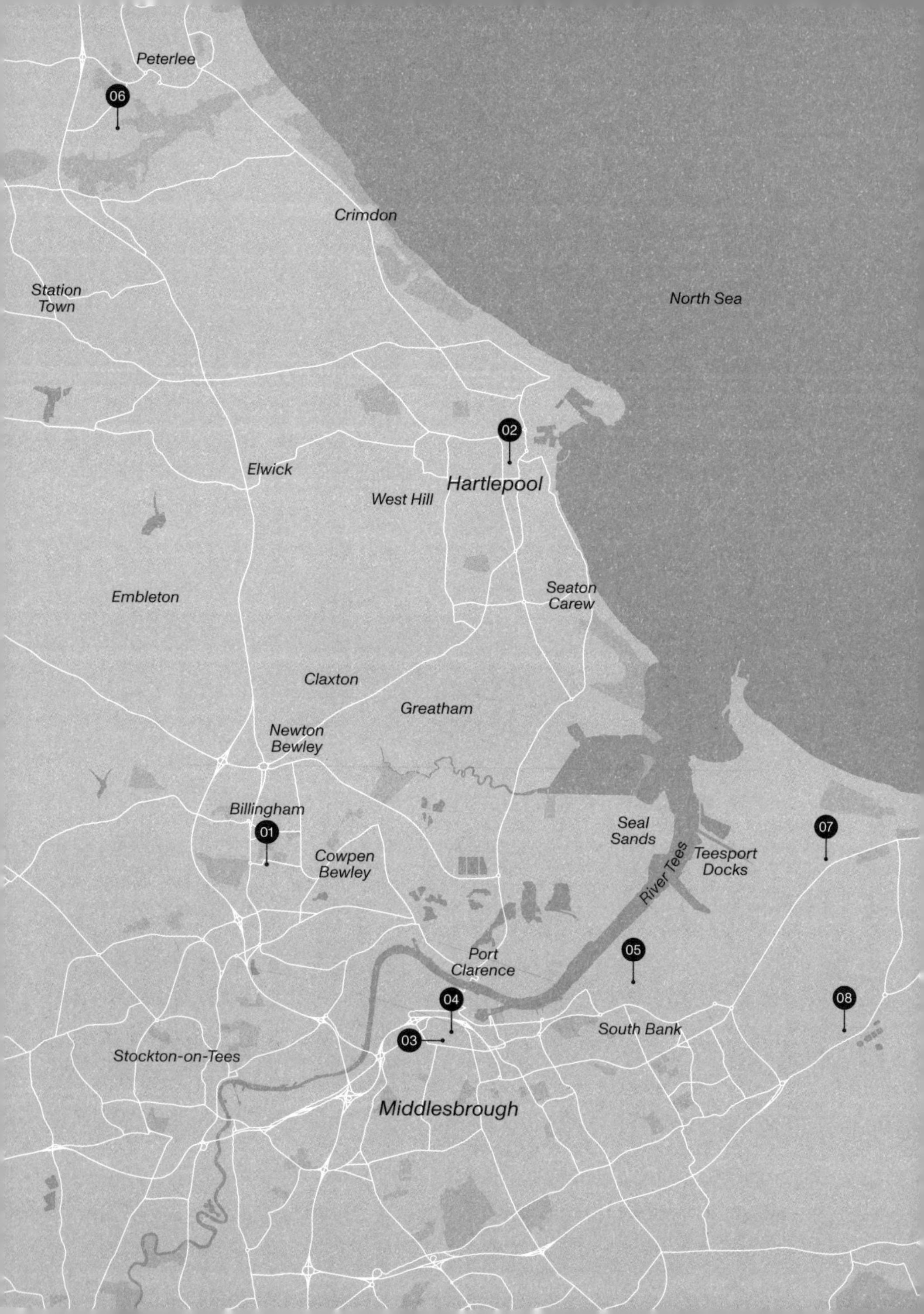

Peterlee
06
Crimdon
Station
Town
North Sea
02
Elwick
Hartlepool
West Hill
Embleton
Seaton
Carew
Claxton
Greatham
Newton
Bewley
Billingham
01
Cowpen
Bewley
Seal
Sands
River Tees
Teesport
Docks
07
05
Port
Clarence
04
08
03
South Bank
Stockton-on-Tees
Middlesbrough

North East

Middlesbrough & Hartlepool

Billingham Town Centre, 1961–67

Hartlepool Civic Centre, 1973–76

← Middlesbrough, Church House, 1974

↑ Middlesbrough Civic Centre, 1971–73

Middlesbrough, Dorman Long Tower, 1954–57

Peterlee, Apollo Pavilion, 1969

Redcar, Steel House, 1977

Redcar, Wilton Centre, 1975

Cramlington
Seaton Delaval
North Sea
Burradon
West Holywell
Earsdon
Whitley Bay
High Gosforth Park
Killingworth
Murton Village
Tynemouth
North Shields
Gosforth
South Shields
Jesmond
Wallsend
Newcastle upon Tyne
River Tyne
Jarrow
Hebburn
Gateshead
Cleadon
East Boldon
Lamesley
River Wear
Sunderland
Washington
A1(M)
Picktree
01
02
03
04
05
06
07
08
09
10
11
12
13
14
15
16
17
18
19
20
21
22
23
24

North East

Newcastle & Sunderland

01 Cramlington, Sterling Organics
02 Gateshead, Crowhall Towers
03 Gateshead Police Station
04 Newcastle, Byker Wall
05 Newcastle, Byker Viaduct
06 Newcastle Civic Centre
07 Newcastle, Claremont Complex
08 Newcastle, Engineering Research Station for British Gas
09 Newcastle, Hadrian Bridge
10 Newcastle, Herschel Building
11 Newcastle, Jesmond Library
12 Newcastle, Hadrian Building
13 Newcastle, Manors Car Park
14 Newcastle, MEA House
15 Newcastle, Robinson Library
16 Newcastle, Salvation Army Men's Social Services Centre
17 Newcastle, Shieldfield House
18 Newcastle, St James' Park
19 Newcastle, Swan House
20 Sunderland, Town Central Area
21 Sunderland Civic Centre
22 Sunderland, Salvation Army – Swan Lodge Lifehouse
23 Washington, Edith Avenue
24 Whitley Bay, Beacon House

← Cramlington, Sterling Organics, 1972

↑ Gateshead, Crowhall Towers, 1966–68

Gateshead Police Station, 1971–72

Newcastle, Byker Wall, 1969–82

Newcastle, Byker Viaduct, 1976–79

Newcastle Civic Centre, 1956–67

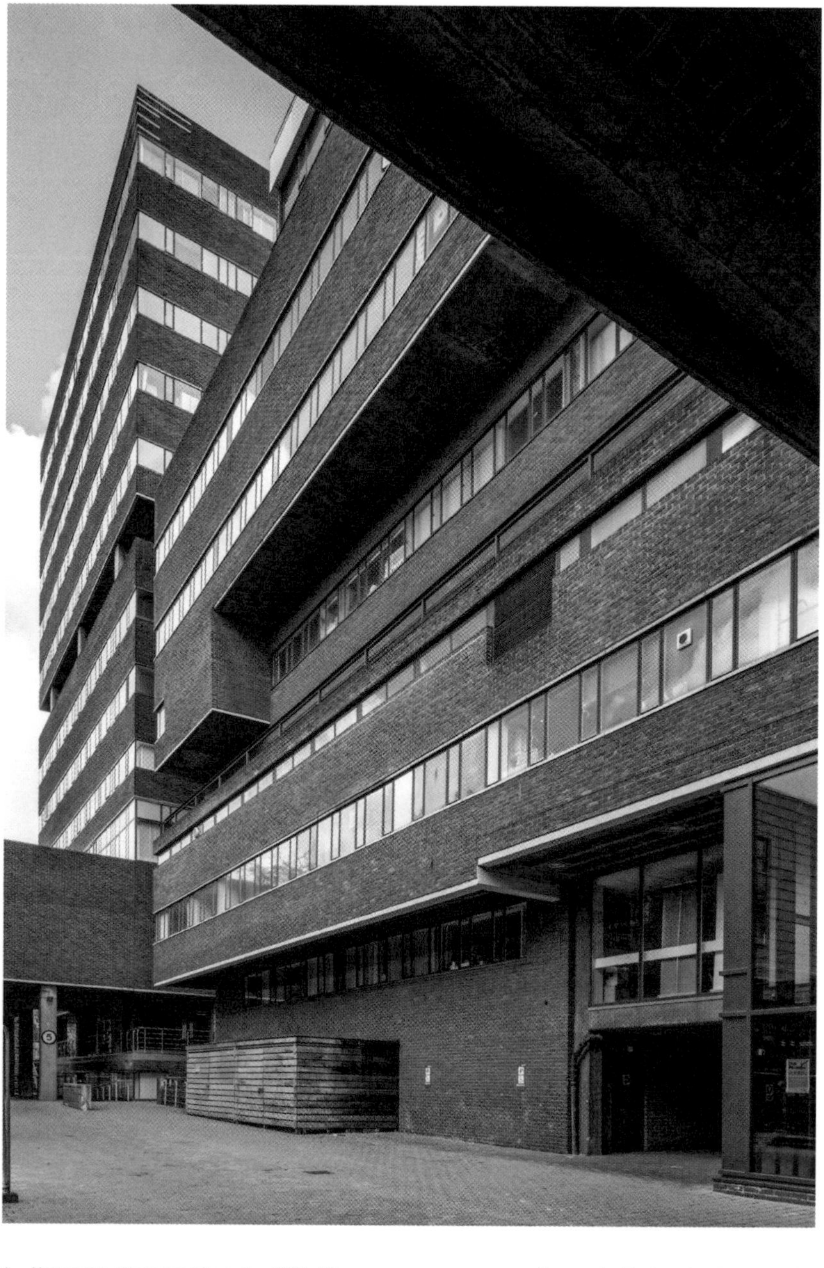

↑ Newcastle, Claremont Complex, 1965–68

→ Newcastle, Engineering Research Station, 1966–67

← Newcastle, Hadrian Bridge, 1975

↑ Newcastle, Herschel Building, 1957–62

Newcastle, Jesmond Library, 1962–63

Newcastle, Hadrian Building, formerly King's Road Centre, 1960–64

Newcastle, Manors Car Park, 1969

Newcastle, MEA House, 1972–74

Newcastle, Robinson Library, 1980–82

Newcastle, Salvation Army Men's Social Services Centre, 1972–74

Newcastle, Shieldfield House, 1967

→ Newcastle, St James' Park, 1972–73

YOU ARE HERE

NA17 XTU

Newcastle, Swan House, 1967–69

↑ Sunderland, Town Central Area, 1967–69

→ Sunderland Civic Centre, 1965

FIRE EXIT
NO PARKING THIS SIDE

← Sunderland, Salvation Army, 1982

↑ Washington, Edith Avenue, 1964–69

Whitley Bay, Beacon House, 1962

M58
M57
Aintree
Rimrose Valley Country Park
West Park
St Helens
14
13
Ravenhead
New Hall
03
M57
Bootle
11
Stanley Park
Anfield
Everton
Knotty Ash
09
04
Liverpool
07
08
06
01
02
05
12
10
M62
Toxteth
Belle Vale
Princess Park
Calderstones Park
River Mersey

North West

Merseyside & Wirral

01 Liverpool, Dental School
02 Liverpool, Dept of Electrical Engineering & Electronics
03 Liverpool, Fire Training Centre
04 Liverpool, Kingsway Tunnel Vents
05 Liverpool, Metropolitan Cathedral of Christ the King
06 Liverpool, Queen Elizabeth II Law Courts
07 Liverpool, Former headquarters of Royal Insurance
08 Liverpool, Royal University Hospital
09 Liverpool, Sculptural Wall
10 Liverpool, Sydney Jones Library
11 Liverpool, Tate & Lyle Sugar Silo
12 Liverpool, University Sports and Fitness Centre
13 St Helens, Former headquarters of Pilkington Glass
14 St Helens, Ormskirk Street United Reformed Church

Liverpool, Dental School, 1963–78

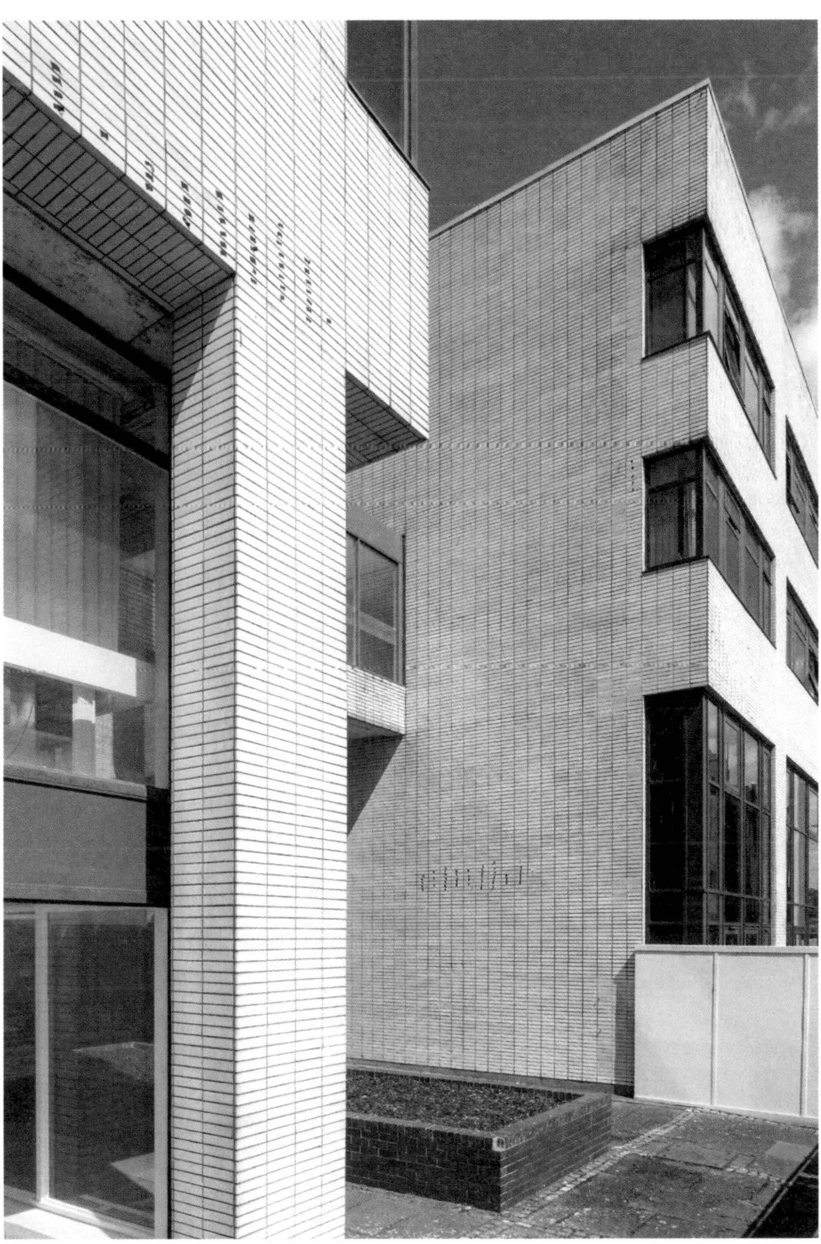

Liverpool, Department of Electrical Engineering and Electronics, 1962–65

Liverpool, Fire Training Centre, 1967

Liverpool, Kingsway Tunnel Vents, 1966–71

Liverpool, Metropolitan Cathedral of Christ the King, 1962–67

Liverpool, Queen Elizabeth II Law Courts, 1979–84

Liverpool, Former headquarters of Royal Insurance, 1974–76

Liverpool, Royal University Hospital, 1963–78

← Liverpool, Sculptural Wall, 1962

↑ Liverpool, Sydney Jones Library, 1974–76

Liverpool, Tate & Lyle Sugar Silo, 1955–57

Liverpool, University Sports and Fitness Centre, 1963–66

St Helens, Former headquarters of Pilkington Glass, 1959–63

St Helens, Ormskirk Street United Reformed Church, 1976

15
Rochdale
M62
Bury
M66
Castleton
13
M62
14
Oldha
Heaton Park
M60
M61
01
Drinkwater Park
18
Swinton
17
Cheetham Hill
04
M60
M602
Salford
Manchester
10
02
Manchester Ship Canal
08
07
Ordsall
Salford Quays
06
09
Audenshaw Reservoirs
Old Trafford
03
11
05
Rusholme
Longsight
12
Whalley Range
Stretford
M60
River Mersey
Reddish Vale Country Park
M60
Stockport
16

North West

Greater Manchester

01 Blackley, Hexagon Tower
02 Manchester, Barnes Wallis Building
03 Manchester, Church of the Ascension
04 Manchester, CIS Tower
05 Manchester, Ellen Wilkinson Humanities Building
06 Manchester, Extension to John Dalton Building
07 Manchester, Maths and Social Sciences Building
08 Manchester, Oxford Road Station
09 Manchester, Precinct Centre
10 Manchester, Renold Building
11 Manchester, St Augustine RC Church
12 Manchester, Domestic and Trades College ('Toastrack')
13 Middleton, Hopwood Hall Chapel
14 Oldham Civic Centre
15 Rochdale, College Bank Estate
16 Stockport, Stopford House
17 Swinton Civic Centre
18 Swinton, Lancastrian Hall and Central Library

Blackley, Hexagon Tower, 1971

Manchester, Barnes Wallis Building, 1963–66

Manchester, Church of the Ascension, 1970

Manchester, CIS Tower, 1959–62

Manchester, Ellen Wilkinson Humanities Building, 1964

Manchester, Extension to John Dalton Building, 1974

Manchester, Maths and Social Sciences Building, 1968

Manchester, Oxford Road Station, 1960

Manchester, Precinct Centre, 1970–72

Manchester, Renold Building, 1960–62

Manchester, St Augustine RC Church, 1967–68

Manchester, Domestic and Trades College ('Toastrack'), 1958–60

Middleton, Hopwood Hall Chapel, 1964–65

Oldham Civic Centre, 1975–77

Rochdale, College Bank Estate, 1965–70

Stockport, Stopford House, 1975

← Swinton Civic Centre, 1973

Swinton, Lancastrian Hall and Central Library, 1968

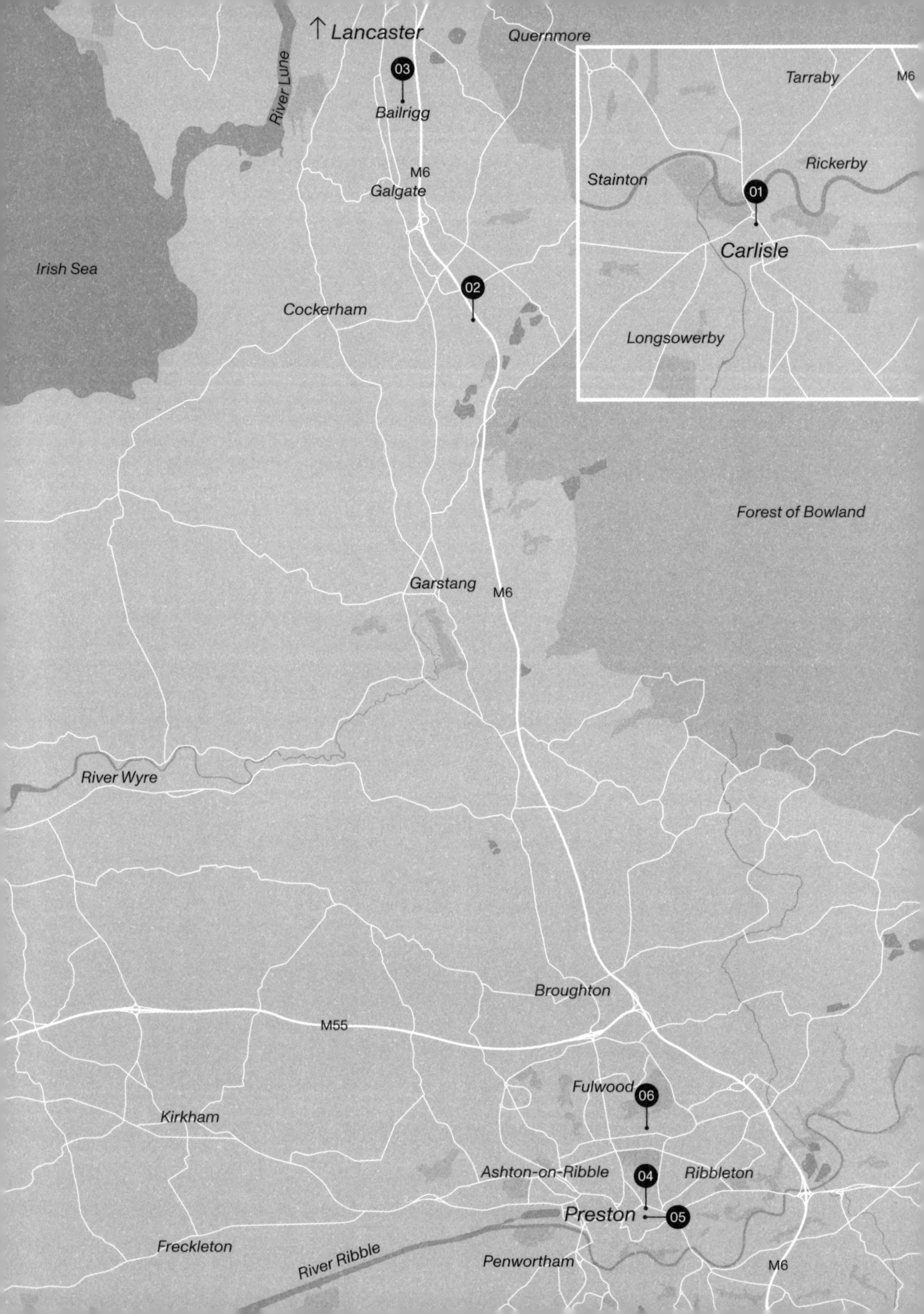

↑ Lancaster
Quernmore
River Lune
03
Bailrigg
M6
Galgate
Irish Sea
02
Cockerham
Tarraby
M6
Stainton
Rickerby
01
Carlisle
Longsowerby
Forest of Bowland
Garstang
M6
River Wyre
Broughton
M55
Fulwood
06
Kirkham
Ashton-on-Ribble
04
Ribbleton
Preston
05
Freckleton
River Ribble
Penwortham
M6

North West

Cumbria & Lancashire

01 Carlisle Civic Centre
02 Lancaster, Forton Services
03 Lancaster, University Chaplaincy
04 Preston Central Bus Station and Car Park
05 Preston Guild Hall
06 Preston, Kennington Primary School

Carlisle Civic Centre, 1964

Lancaster, Forton Services, 1964–65

Lancaster, University Chaplaincy Centre, 1969

Preston Central Bus Station and Car Park, 1968–69

Preston Guild Hall, 1969–73

Preston, Kennington Primary School, 1973–74

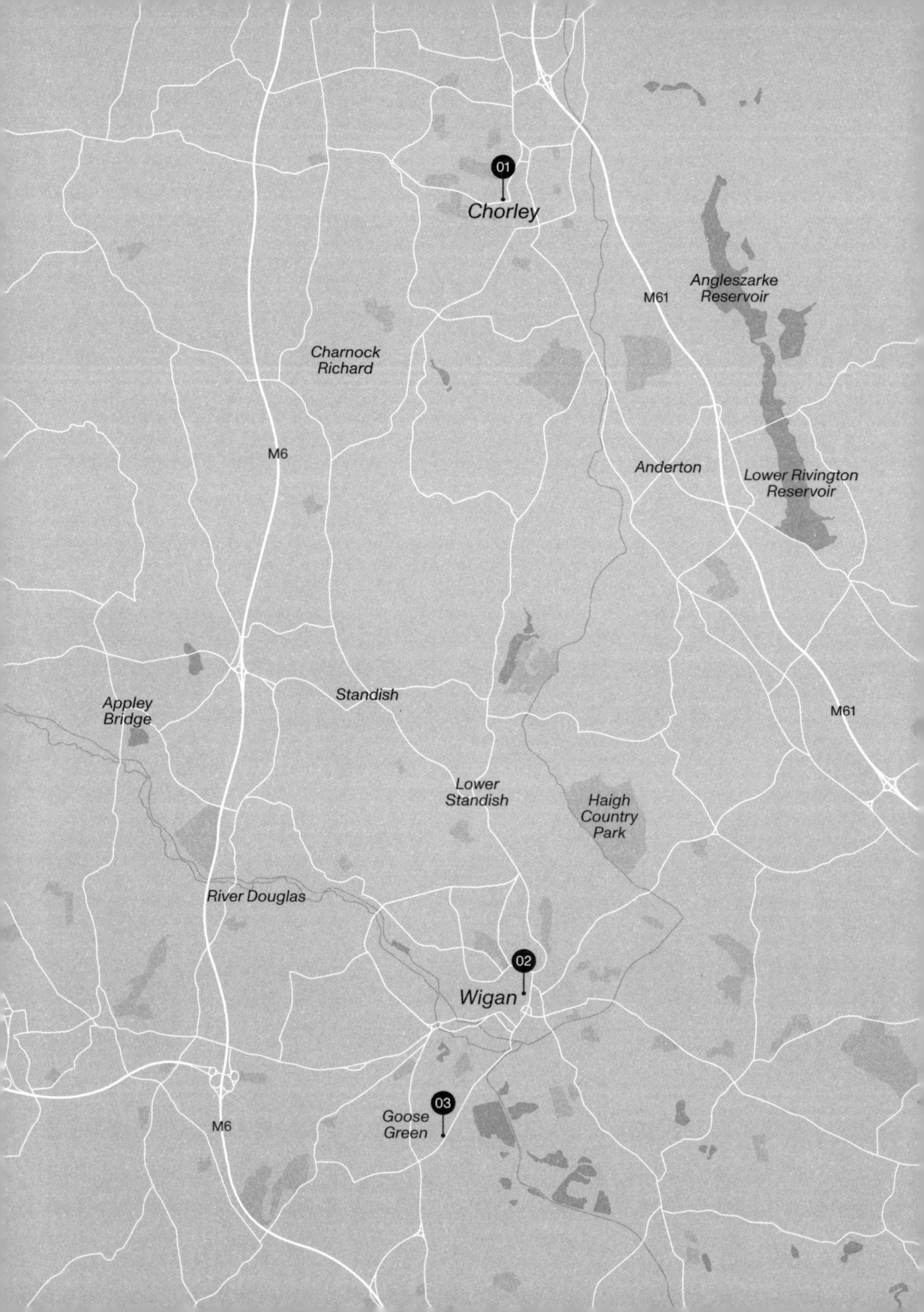

01
Chorley
M61
Angleszarke
Reservoir
Charnock
Richard
M6
Anderton
Lower Rivington
Reservoir
Standish
Appley
Bridge
M61
Lower
Standish
Haigh
Country
Park
River Douglas
02
Wigan
03
Goose
Green
M6

North West

Chorley & Wigan

01 Chorley Police Station
02 Wigan Civic Centre
03 Wigan, St Jude RC Church

Chorley Police Station, 1968

Wigan Civic Centre, 1970

Wigan, St Jude RC Church, 1964–65

Building Information

by Matthew Steele

Building information is alphabetical by town and then building name within each region. Page numbers given under buildings indicate the main photo.

Central Telephone Exchange, Sharpe Street, Bradford BD5
Designed by TH Anson
Built 1976, not listed, P.020

↑ Central Telephone Exchange is a five-storey extension to the old Manchester Road Exchange, and occupies a site bounded by Sharpe Street to the north and Burrow Street to the south. The building was commissioned in 1970 by the newly formed Department of the Environment. The structure is reinforced concrete with non-structural pre-cast concrete panels, both fairfaced and ribbed. Three stair cores adds visual interest to an otherwise uncompromising building.

High Point, Westgate, Bradford BD1
Designed by John Tempest for the John Brunton Partnership
Built 1972, not listed, P.021

↑ Originally known as Permanent House, this eight-storey ribbed concrete building was the headquarters of the Bradford Building Society until, following mergers with the Huddersfield Building Society in 1975 and West Yorkshire Building Society in 1982, it became home to the newly formed Yorkshire Building Society. Subsequently known as High Point, the building was designed by John Brunton Partnership. A large-format colour image of Bolton Abbey, West Yorkshire, was commissioned for the reception, and hand-finished by AH Leach and Co of Brighouse, one of Britain's oldest photographic laboratories.

Kirkgate Centre, Kirkgate, Bradford BD1
Designed by John Brunton Partnership
Built 1974, not listed, P.022

↑ Opened as Kirkgate Arndale Centre in 1974, the building was controversial for more than one reason. Firstly, its construction required the demolition of the old Kirkgate Market (1872) by Lockwood and Mawson – a move that was keenly contested by Kirkgate Market Action Group. More controversial though was its association with the disgraced architect-planner John Poulson. Poulson had fostered relationships with both Bradford City Council and the Arndale Property Trust, and even developed his own proposals for the site. Jailed for bribing officials in 1974, the commission was awarded to the Bradford-based practice of John Brunton Partnership whose earlier work included High Point (see above). The Kirkgate Centre is a multi-level structure of ribbed concrete containing a series of concrete murals, possibly by the artist William Mitchell. Thirteen fibre-glass murals were created by Mitchell for another John Brunton Partnership building – the headquarters of the Bradford and Bingley Building Society (1972–74), Bingley, which was demolished in 2015.

Doncaster Magistrates' Court and Police Station, College Road, Doncaster DN1
Designed by Frederick Gibberd and Partners with LJ Tucker
Built 1969, not listed, P.056

↑ In 1954, plans were drawn up by Sir Frederick Gibberd, Doncaster's appointed architect-planner, for a new Civic Centre. Along with new law courts and police station, a pedestrianised shopping centre and town hall were proposed. The town hall never materialised and the shopping centre, once built, was fraught with financial difficulties. The law courts and police station, however, were deemed worthy of mention by the judges of the 1970 Concrete Society Award. Given the diversity of form, colour and texture of existing neighbouring buildings, external materials were limited to polished pre-cast concrete panels with aluminium-framed glazing. Arranged around a large top-lit concourse, general accommodation occupies the ground floor of the law courts, while the courts themselves – seven in number – are at first floor. An underground passage runs from the basement through to the police station.

Elim Pentecostal Church, Hall Street, Halifax HX1
Designed by CS Oldfield with RW Wands
of Rainham Timber Engineering
Built 1972, not listed, P.024

↑ Erected on land east of Burdock Way, Elim Pentecostal Church was built on the site of a former depot. The main worshipping space is square on plan and has a roof comprised of 48 folded timber panels. It is connected to the ancillary accommodation via an entrance canopy reminiscent of Basil Spence's Coventry Cathedral (1962). Construction is mainly smooth-faced pre-cast concrete with some brickwork infill. A faceted mural to the right of the entrance, while of the appearance of being concrete, is possibly fibreglass or treated timber.

Haley Court, Range Lane, Halifax H3
Designed by Vincent, Gorbing and Partners
Built 1968, not listed, P.025

↑ Not dissimilar to the H-plan tower blocks by Gillinson, Barnett and Partners in Leeds (see Marlborough Towers, below), Haley Court was commissioned by Halifax County Borough Council and is comprised of three towers: Haley Court, Range Court and Akroyd Court. Each contains 85 individual dwellings with a structural frame of reinforced concrete and brown brick infill.

Halifax Building, Trinity Road, Halifax HX1
Designed by Building Design Partnership
Built 1968–74, listed grade II, P.023

↑ The Halifax Building was designed by Building Design Partnership as the new headquarters of the Halifax Building Society. It was planned according to Bürolandschaft principles, an approach developed in Germany in the 1950s to promote a more social and collaborative work environment. Accordingly, from the entrance hall one could access a mezzanine level with facilities which included a restaurant, games rooms, and a bar. The upper levels are an irregular quadrilateral shape, as dictated by site constraints, and are open plan – a feat made possible owing to a four-metre-deep truss at second floor. All floors are connected by a central core and four corner staircases, each faced externally with York stone above roof level. Elsewhere, infill is brown anodised aluminium framing with opaque brown glass spandrels.

Humber Bridge, Hessle, East Yorkshire HU13
Designed by Freeman Fox and Partners with RE Slater
Built 1973–81, listed grade I, P.032

↑ Until the opening of the Humber Bridge in 1981, passage over the river was by boat only. At 1,410 metres in length, it was longest single-span bridge in the world at the time of construction and was designed by Freeman Fox and Partners, the engineers also responsible for the Forth Road Bridge and the Severn Bridge. Unlike those examples, which were built in steel, the Humber Bridge was technologically innovative in its use of reinforced concrete to overcome challenging geomorphological conditions. Upon designation of its grade I listed status, Historic England referred to its 'taut, pared-down elegance'.

Central Services Building, University of Huddersfield, Queensgate, Huddersfield HD1
Designed by Wilson and Womersley
Built 1973–77, not listed, P.026

↑ Following the establishment of Huddersfield Polytechnic in 1970, a masterplan for expansion was put forward by Wilson and Womersley which proposed a central facilities building to act as a spine of the developing campus. Subsequently commissioned to undertake its design, the building is of in situ cast reinforced concrete, with coffered slabs and circular columns. Externally, the pale buff-coloured bricks were chosen to mimic the local sandstone.

Midland Bank, Cloth Hall Street, Huddersfield HD1
Designed by Peter Womersley, Kitson and Partners
Built 1970, not listed, P.027

↑ Located on a restricted site, this five-storey building is comprised of a double-height banking hall with mezzanine, above which are four storeys of office and storage accommodation. The exposed concrete columns and double projecting beams are bush hammered, and carry a facade of smooth brown granite cladding and bronze anodised aluminium glazing. Originally the banking hall featured a dark mustard-coloured carpet, rosewood joinery and cream leather seating to give an air of luxury to this publicly accessible space.

Queensgate Market, Princess Alexandra Walk, Huddersfield HD1
Designed by Gwyn Roberts of J Seymour Harris Partnership
Built 1968–70, listed Grade II, P.028

↑ This rectangular structure is noted for its innovative roof, which, supported by 21 mushroom-headed concrete columns, is comprised of individual asymmetrical concrete sections with board-marked soffits. The intention was to replicate the canopies of traditional outdoor markets. Vertical infill between each roof section is provided by top-hung aluminium glazing with concertinaed rubber membranes acting as both a seal and movement joint. Another distinguishing feature is the ten-part ceramic mural *Articulation in Movement* by the German-born artist Fritz Steller.

Brynmor Jones Library, University of Hull,
Cottingham Road, Hull HU6
Designed by Forsyth and Partners/Castle Park Dean Hook
Built 1956–69, not listed, P.033

↑ Brynmor Jones Library is the former workplace of the poet Philip Larkin, who acted as chief librarian from 1955 until his death in 1985. Larkin was involved in both the initial planning and subsequent expansion of the library. The first phase of the library opened in 1956 and, designed by Forsyth and Partners, is a red brick building with Art Deco flourishes in keeping with earlier campus buildings by the same firm in the 1920s and 1930s. As the university itself expanded, subsequent to the Martin Plan of 1967 (see below), a second phase of construction saw an eight-storey steel-framed extension erected with pre-cast concrete panels and glazed infill. Designed by Castle Park Dean and Hook, it was completed in 1969. Redevelopment and refurbishment work was carried out by Sheppard Robson in 2015.

Gulbenkian Centre, University of Hull,
Cottingham Road, Hull HU6
Designed by Peter Moro with Michael Heard
Built 1967–69, listed grade II, P.034

↑ The Gulbenkian Centre was constructed as part of an expansion plan prepared by the architect Leslie Martin in 1967 for University of Hull. Purpose-built for the drama department, it is octagonal on plan, and its construction is of red brick and board-marked concrete with a copper-clad roof. The performance space includes flexible seating, in keeping with Moro's experimentations in theatre design. Similarly, the drama studio, which is positioned at the centre of the building, is unadorned in order to promote flexibility.

Kingston House, Bond Street, Hull HU1
Designed by Fry, Drew and Partners
Built 1965–67, not listed, P.035

↑ Kingston House was designed to house the offices of Humberside County Council, and is by the renowned practice of Fry, Drew and Partners. Maxwell Fry who is, perhaps, better known for his residential projects of the interwar years, such as Sun House (1935) and Kensal House Flats (1937) in London, provided the council with a low-rise three-storey block above which rises a twelve-storey tower. It is a concrete-framed structure from which pre-cast concrete panels are hung. Despite calls for its demolition, the building was refurbished between 2017 and 2018, and now contains a hotel, office space and private apartments.

The Lawns, University of Hull, Harland Way, Cottingham, Hull HU16
Designed by Gillespie Kidd and Coia
Built 1963–68, listed grade II*, P.036

↑ The Lawns were purpose-built student halls of residence commissioned by the University of Hull, and located several miles away from the campus outside the village of Cottingham. Originally, the scheme consisted of 12 self-contained units but, in the end, only six were constructed. The six units were arranged around a central lawn and a self-service restaurant, while the provision of an internal courtyard for each individual unit was intended to engender greater independence. The Lawns was closed in 2018 due to falling demand and is now being used by Humberside Police for firearms training

Sports Centre, University of Hull, Inglemire Lane, Hull HU6
Designed by Peter Womersley
Built 1963–65, listed grade II, P.038

↑ Born in Yorkshire and residing in the Scottish Borders, Peter Womersley was one of the foremost British modernist architects and well-known among his contemporaries for bringing modernist designs to the smaller towns and cities of Britain. He designed all manner of building types from houses and studios to boiler houses and football stadia. For the University of Hull, Womersley turned his hand to a sports centre and produced an elegant structure which evokes, but does not imitate, the work of the Brazilian architect Oscar Niemeyer: narrow windows are set in concrete mullions around the perimeter to bring natural light into the central space.

Tidal Surge Barrier, Humber Street, Hull HU1
Designed by Oliver Cox of Shankland Cox Associates
Built 1977–80, listed grade II, P.037

↑ The Tidal Surge Barrier, located at the confluence of the River Hull and the Humber estuary, was commissioned by Yorkshire Water Authority following severe flooding to the city of Hull in 1969. Although flood defences are often entirely functional constructions, Tidal Surge Barrier is sculptural too. The 30-metre barrier gate is supported by two concrete towers with curtain wall glazing to the stairwells. Oliver Cox, partner-in-charge at Shankland Cox Associates, worked with the engineering firm Sir M McDonald and Partners to ensure the correct fit between the tidal barrier design and the machinery required within. The barrier gate turns 90 degrees to allow large ships to navigate their way through.

Wilberforce Building, Cottingham Road, Hull HU6
Designed by Napper, Errington, Collerton, Barnett, Allott
Built 1968–70, not listed, P.039

↑ Many of the University of Hull's pre-1960 campus buildings were of red brick. The Wilberforce Building, along with the Gulbenkian Centre and extension to Brynmor Jones Library (above), represented a departure from this, as the university's expansion plans gathered pace. Designed by Napper, Errington, Collerton, Barnett, Allott, it has a reinforced concrete frame, cast in situ, with pre-cast concrete cladding panels. Although Jack Hollingworth Napper had taught alongside Leslie Martin at the Hull School of Architecture in the 1930s, the partner in charge was J Errington with CJ Rainford acting as project architect.

Bank House, King Street, Leeds LS1
Designed by Building Design Partnership
Built 1969–71, listed grade II, P.042

↑ Founded in 1961 by George Grenfell-Baines, Building Design Partnership was conceived as the world's first interdisciplinary practice (see also Worsley Medical and Dental Building, Leeds, and Halifax Building, Halifax). Bank House, completed just ten years later, is an exemplar of the firm's ambition to apply complex engineering solutions to its own designs. The building is square on plan and, at five storeys in height, adopts the form of an inverted ziggurat with a central light well penetrating the top two floors. It is of in situ cast reinforced concrete construction, clad in grey granite and bronze. A sculptured aluminium ceiling by the artist Alan Boyson has since been removed.

Campus Expansion, University of Leeds, Leeds LS2
Designed by Chamberlin, Powell and Bon
Built 1963–78, not listed, P.048

↑ In 1959, Chamberlin, Powell and Bon were selected from a shortlist of just four candidates to oversee the expansion of Leeds University; the others being Denys Lasdun, James Stirling and Bill Howell. The plan aimed to encourage a collegiate atmosphere by providing high-density student accommodation along with a centrally located building to house pooled lecture theatres. The practice subsequently designed several of the new campus's buildings including interconnected teaching buildings for Mathematics (1966), Physics (1968), Biology (1968) and Biophysics (1969), a lecture theatre block (Roger Stevens Building, below) and the Edward Boyle Library (1975). The commission for a new medical school (Worsley Medical and Dental Building) was passed on to Building Design Partnership.

Combined Court Centre, Oxford Row, Leeds LS1
Designed by Property Services Agency
Built 1982, not listed, P.044

↑ One of several combined courts erected in the first half of the decade, such buildings are indicative of a shift from the imposing courthouses of the Victorian period towards something more civic; Burnley Combined Court (1981), for example, was clad in a tile not dissimilar to Manchester's Arndale Shopping Centre (1972–79). In Leeds, the building is red brick with an aesthetic redolent of a 1970s leisure centre.

Marlborough Towers, Marlborough Street, Leeds LS1
Designed by Gillinson, Barnett and Partners
Built 1963–66, not listed, P.045

↑ One of several near-identical H-plan tower blocks designed by Gillinson, Barnett and Partners for Leeds County Borough Council and erected in the 1960s; others include Holborn Tower, Burnsall Grange and Burnsall Croft. Marlborough Towers has 17 storeys containing 99 individual dwellings. The structural frame is reinforced concrete, with hollow-pot floors and brick infill.

Roger Stevens Building, University of Leeds, Woodhouse, Leeds LS2
Designed by Chamberlin, Powell and Bon
Built 1968–71, listed grade II*, PP.046–047

↑ The Roger Stevens Building was erected to house multiple lecture theatres, and acts as a focal point of Leeds University's expanding campus. An initial design prepared by Joe Chamberlin, along with team member Daryl Jackson, was abandoned in 1963, its cantilevered theatres deemed too expensive by the funding University Grants Commission. However, with the Robbins Report that same year calling for the mass expansion of higher education, the scheme was revisited. New team member Douglas Jackson proposed ramped circulation in order to eliminate the need for cantilevers and, at ground level beneath the largest theatre, another team member, David Ford, designed a café space. Simplified thus, the building went ahead. Constructed of reinforced concrete, since painted, its character is derived from the ventilation pipes and recessed balconies to the west elevation.

University Centre, Leeds City College, Park Lane, Leeds LS3
Architect unknown
Built 1970s, not listed, P.043

↑ University Centre was established by Leeds City College at the former College House to provide undergraduate study, professional courses and degree-level apprenticeships. The building appears to have been erected speculatively in the 1970s, and was originally called Concord House.

Worsley Medical and Dental Building, University of Leeds, Clarendon Way, Leeds LS2
Designed by Building Design Partnership
Built 1976–79, not listed, P.049

↑ The Medical and Dental Building at the University of Leeds had a long gestation period. Considered an integral part of the campus masterplan previously devised by the firm Chamberlin, Powell and Bon, the commission was, nonetheless, handed to Building Design Partnership who from 1962 onwards engaged with representatives from United Leeds Hospitals and the Council of the University to develop the brief. Containing a Dental Hospital, a School of Dentistry, a lecture theatre, library and laboratories, the as-built design was compact in form and deep in plan. The sculpted concrete facade owes much to the practice's earlier work at Preston Central Bus Station and Car Park (1968–69), both buildings being products of their Preston office.

Beeversleigh Flats, Clifton Lane, Rotherham S65
Designed by Maurice Dakin of Gillinson Barnett and Partners
Built 1970–71, not listed, P.057

↑ Leeds-based Gillinson Barnett and Partners designed several housing schemes around Yorkshire including Marlborough Towers, Leeds (above), St Ann's, Rotherham (1969) and The Lanes, Rotherham (1970), the latter among the highly commended schemes at the 1970 Good Design in Housing Awards. Commissioned by Rotherham County Borough Council, Beeversleigh Flats is a 13-storey hexagonal block with cantilever balconies on all side. It has a smooth-faced reinforced concrete frame with red brick infill matching the neighbouring houses. The practice also designed Rotherham's Herringthorpe Leisure Centre (1974), which was demolished in 2009.

Fire Training Centre at Rotherham Fire Station, Fitzwilliam Road, Rotherham S65
Architect unknown
Date unknown, not listed, PP.058–059

↑ Facing onto Fitzwilliam Road, Rotherham Fire Station is itself pretty unremarkable. Located to the rear, however, is a standalone training and development centre where both firefighters and cadets alike can tackle real fires and practise evacuation drills. The structure is concrete and brick, both being non-combustible materials.

Pumping Station, Marsh Street, Rotherham S60
Architect unknown
Date unknown, not listed, PP.060–061

↑ Located next to the River Don, very little information is known about this pump house. Constructed from pre-cast concrete panels, vertically ribbed, it was possibly commissioned by the Environment Agency.

Arts Tower, Faculty of Arts, Economics and Social Studies, University of Sheffield, Bolsover Street, Sheffield S3
Designed by Gollins Melvin Ward Partnership
Built 1962–65, listed grade II*, P.062

↑ The University of Sheffield's redevelopment plans, prepared by Gollins Melvin Ward Partnership in 1953, called for a focal point to the campus; a role that would be fulfilled by the high-rise tower built to house the Faculty of Arts, Economics and Social Studies. At 18 storeys in height, the ground-floor podium contains an entrance lobby with mezzanine level. From here, a covered walkway links the faculty to Western Bank Library (1959), an earlier building by the firm (see below).

Pooled lecture theatres can be found on the lower-ground levels, while on the upper levels, faculty departments are grouped over multiple floors. A circulation and services core occupies the centre of the building, with a paternoster lift running from the lower-ground level to the 13th floor.

Crucible Theatre, Norfolk Street, Sheffield S1
Designed by Nicholas Thompson and Robin Benyon of Renton Howard Wood Levin
Built 1969–71, listed grade II, P.063

↑ Developed in consultation with theatre designer Tanya Moiseiwitsch, the Crucible Theatre incorporates backstage workshops, rehearsal rooms and dressing rooms. The auditorium is a sound-proofed octagon with pre-cast concrete seating units supported by an in situ cast concrete slab. Outside of the auditorium, varnished free-standing concrete columns repeat the octagonal form of the auditorium. Fortlcrete limestone masonry blocks are used throughout: grey backstage and white for public areas and external walls.

Department of Geography, University of Sheffield, Winter Street, Sheffield S3
Designed by David Lyle of William Whitfield and Partners
Built 1970–71, not listed, P.064

↑ Located behind the University of Sheffield's Western Bank Library (see below) is the Department of Geography, designed by William Whitfield and Partners. Originally scheduled for construction in the latter half of the 1960s, funding delays meant the project was not completed until 1971. The building is comprised of seven hexagonal structures which house lecture theatres, reading rooms, and an exhibition and museum space. A rectangular three-storey teaching block is accessed from a centrally located lift and stair core. Construction throughout is of reinforced concrete frames with pale brown brick infill.

Electricity Substation, Moore Street, Sheffield S3
Designed by Bryan Jefferson of Jefferson Sheard and Partners
Built 1968, listed grade II, P.068

↑ Bryan Jefferson founded his Sheffield-based practice with Gerry Sheard in 1958, and the firm designed several buildings around the city including the Cinema and Entertainment Complex on Pond Street (below) and Moore Street Electricity Substation. A collaboration with the Civil Engineers' Department of the Central Electricity Generating Board (North East Region), the substation is rectangular on plan, albeit chamfered at the south-west end. The structure is comprised of a reinforced concrete portal frame with infill of dark grey brick at ground level, and exposed aggregate concrete panels on the two upper levels. The ground floor houses two transformers, with switch gear occupying the floor above. The second floor, now empty, once contained busbars linked to the switchgear below. Vertical circulation is via an external staircase with covered walkways at the north-east end of the building.

Gleadless Valley Estate, Sheffield S14
Designed by Sheffield City Architects' Department (under John Lewis Womersley)
Built 1955–62, not listed, P.065

↑ Serving as city architect between 1953 and 1964, and prior to joining Leslie Hugh Wilson in private partnership, John Lewis Womersley's ambition was to bring order to the ad hoc nineteenth-century development which characterised much of Sheffield. As well as new housing in the central areas of Netherthorpe and Park Hill (see below), further development took place at Greenhill-Bradway and Gleadless Valley. Five miles south of the city centre, the Gleadless Valley Estate included a variety of house types of varying colours, with pathways through retained woodland intended to create a sense of individual villages. As well as housing, the development included schools, shops, public houses and churches (see below).

Holy Cross Church, Spotswood Mount,
Gleadless Valley, Sheffield S14
Designed by Braddock and Martin Smith
Built 1964–65, not listed, P.066

↑ With the population of Sheffield Corporation's Gleadless Valley Estate growing throughout the 1950s, competitive church-building soon followed. The first place to open was Gleadless Valley Methodist Church, Blackstock Road (1960), designed by J Mansell Jenkinson and Son. This was followed by the rather unassuming St Anthony's RC Church, Sandby Drive (1963). A late-comer to the estate, the Anglicans announced their presence with the highly distinctive Holy Cross. From its elevated hillside position, a white concrete crucifix at the roof's apex looms over the houses below. The form of the nave offers the congregation greater visibility of the altar than liturgically more traditional churches. Two full-height windows of concrete and glass occupy the west end of the church and, depicting Mary and St John, were designed by the artist John Baker.

Park Hill, bounded by Duke Street,
Talbot Street and South Street, Sheffield S2
Designed by Jack Lynn, Ivor Smith and Frederick Nicklin of Sheffield City Architects' Department
(under John Lewis Womersley)
Built 1958–61, listed grade II*, P.069

↑ Following the demolition of 700 existing houses at Park Hill, the first phase of a central area redevelopment plan, prepared by the city architect Womersley, began in April 1958. The scheme consisted of four interconnected residential blocks with deck access wide enough to accommodate a milk float: as well as shops, other amenities included public houses, launderettes and public toilets. The structural frame is of reinforced concrete, with brick infill and concrete balconies. In accordance with specifications set out by the abstract artist John Forrester, brickwork varies in tone from terracotta and cream to purple and pale red.

Pond Street Entertainment Complex, Pond Street, Sheffield S1
Designed by Bryan Jefferson of Jefferson Sheard and Partners
Built 1965, not listed, P.070

↑ The cinema and entertainment complex on Pond Street was one of the first major commissions in the home city of this Sheffield-based practice, though several others followed including Moore Street Electricity Substation (above) and the extant headquarters of the Amalgamated Engineering Union (1972) on Furnival Street. This large concrete structure contains a multi-storey car park on the lower levels, with shopping and entertainment facilities above. During the late 1970s and 1980s, it was home to Sheffield's much-missed Roxy Disco.

Royal Hallamshire Hospital, Glossop Road,
Broomhall, Sheffield S10
Designed by Adams, Holden and Pearson
Built 1968–78, not listed, P.071

↑ Despite the death of influential founding partner Charles Holden in 1960, the experienced practice of Adams, Holden and Pearson was commissioned to design a replacement building for the soon-to-be-demolished Sheffield Royal Hospital and Sheffield Royal Infirmary; the firm had, in fact, won a competition with the same brief in 1940. The building has two main components: a three-storey out-patients department, which, containing eight purpose-built clinics, was completed in 1969, and the main ward block, which is a 21-storey T-shaped concrete structure accommodating 700 beds.

Sheffield Magistrates' Court, Castle Street, Sheffield S3
Designed by Sheffield City Architects' Department
Built 1978, not listed, P.067

↑ The Magistrates' Court was one of several buildings proposed in 1966 as part of a new Civic Centre by the city architect William Clunie, and subsequently realised under his successor Bernard Warren: other buildings included a theatre (see above), the since-demolished Register Office (1973), referred to locally as the 'Wedding Cake', and the Town Hall extension (1977), otherwise known as the 'Egg Box'. Whereas the Egg Box utilised smooth pre-cast concrete panels, the Magistrates' Court's concrete cladding is almost entirely ribbed. Entered at first-floor level across an open pedestrian footbridge, vertical slit windows on the lower levels lend a fortress-like appearance to the structure.

St Paul's Church, Wordsworth Avenue,
Parsons Cross, Sheffield S5
Designed by Sir Basil Spence
Built 1958–59, listed grade II*, P.072

↑ One of two churches designed by Sir Basil Spence for the Anglican Diocese of Sheffield – the other being St Catherine of Siena, Woodthorpe – St Paul was built to serve Sheffield Corporation's interwar Parsons Cross housing estate. The building is rectangular on plan with a barrel-vaulted roof. The north and south sides of the church are mostly brick with clerestory glazing, while the east and west ends are fully glazed. Internally, the layout is liturgically traditional with benched seating either side of a central aisle. The altar frontal was designed by the architect and son-in-law of Spence, Anthony Blee.

Trinity United Reformed Church, Ecclesall Road, Sheffield S11
Designed by J Mansell Jenkinson and Son
Built 1970–71, not listed, P.073

↑ Following a union between the three Congregational churches of Cemetery Road, Broompark and Endcliffe Park, church member Jenkinson was commissioned to design an enlarged space for the combined congregations. The hall of Endcliffe Park was retained, along with original features including the organ and benched seating, while a new front was added to create Trinity United Reformed Church. Hemmed in between Eccleshall Road and the cliffs of Endcliffe, the newer section of the church is hexagonal on plan and houses a nave faced with concrete blocks. The gold cross above the pulpit is by the Sheffield-born industrial designer David Mellor. The steel cross which adorns the concrete facade, however, was only added in 1989, and sits above three carved roundels taken from the old Cemetery Road church.

Western Bank Library, University of Sheffield,
Western Bank, Sheffield S10
Designed by Gollins Melvin Ward Partnership
Built 1959, listed grade II*, PP.074–075

↑ Western Bank Library was the first building to be completed under redevelopment plans prepared by Gollins Melvin Ward Partnership in 1953 for the central area of the University of Sheffield. Square on plan, an entrance and cataloguing hall provides access to the main reading room, two smaller reading rooms originally designated for post-graduates only, and another reading room housing journals. Whereas the ground-floor perimeter is brick, the first floor is mostly glazed, with Portland stone cladding at floor and eaves level.

Shipley Market, Kirkgate, Shipley BD18
Designed by Shingler Risdon Associates
with Gerald M Baxter
Built 1957–60, not listed, P.029

↑ Built in phases between 1955 and 1960, the redevelopment of Shipley Market was the vision of D Urwin, engineer and surveyor to Shipley Urban District Council. Old shops, houses and lock-ups were cleared away to make space for an open-air market, a large car park and bus terminus, and a building containing 30 new shops. To what extent Urwin was involved in designing the buildings is unclear, but the involvement of the Arndale Property Trust (see Precinct Centre, Manchester, below) brought further expansion including more shops, a public house and a clock tower, the latter a local landmark. These were designed by Shingler Risdon Associates in consultation with the trust's staff architect, Gerald M Baxter.

Assembly Hall, Bootham School, Bootham, York YO30
Designed by Trevor Dannatt
Built 1965–66, listed grade II, P.050

↑ The brief for the school's new assembly hall required that it should function as both a concert hall and theatre and as a place of worship. To be located within the school's existing courtyard, Dannatt's proposal conceived the building as a free-standing sculpture. It is an in situ cast board-marked concrete structure, with clerestory glazing beneath a copper-clad roof. Beyond the entrance foyer is the main hall, gallery and stage. Internal walls are of board-marked concrete, with elm cladding to the gallery parapet. The visual language is similar to Dannatt's Blackheath Quaker Meeting House (1972) in the London Borough of Lewisham.

Central Hall, University of York, University Road, York YO10
Designed by John Speight of Robert Matthew Johnson Marshall and Partners
Built 1966–68, listed grade II, P.051

↑ In 1962, a plan for the University of York was proposed by Robert Matthew Johnson Marshall and Partners that aimed see the student population grow from nothing to 3,000 in just ten years. Erected using the CLASP system of construction, the first two residential colleges – Derwent and Langwith – opened in the autumn of 1965; Central Hall was completed in 1968. Designed as a multi-purpose assembly hall for conferences, lectures and examinations, as well as cultural and ceremonial occasions, large spans meant a reinforced concrete structure was adopted. Broadly hexagonal on plan, the ground floor contains exhibition spaces, while the upper levels, cantilevered over the campus lake, contain the auditorium. The practice also designed the JB Morrell Library, also on campus (see below).

JB Morrell Library, University of York, University Road, York YO10
Designed by Robert Matthew Johnson Marshall and Partners
Built 1965–66, not listed, PP.052–053

↑ Following the new residential blocks and laboratories at the University of York's growing campus was the JB Morrell Library, named after a former Lord Mayor of York who had advocated establishing a university in the city. An early iteration of the design had the library occupying an elevated position overlooking a multi-level car park. However, with finances dictating that the library remain at ground level, the building was pushed back and connected via a footbridge to a car park south of the newly built Heslington Road. Approached from the car park, one encounters a cast aluminium sculpture, Untitled (1967) by the artist Austin Wright. Although the sculpture is listed (at grade II), the building itself is not. Four storeys high, the structural frame is of reinforced concrete with brick and block outer walls. Window frames are aluminium with hardwood surrounds internally.

Billingham Town Centre, County Durham TS23
Designed by Elder Lester and Partners
Built 1961–67, not listed, P.088

↑ Dubbed the 'Miracle of Billingham', Billingham Urban District Council announced plans in 1961 to develop the town along 'New Town' principles without the aid of government funding. Masterplanned by local firm Elder Lester and Partners, the scheme was to be self-financed through local rate charges – a move made possible owing to the presence of Imperial Chemical Industries, a major local employer. Along with several residential blocks, the new town centre was to have a fully pedestrianised shopping precinct, multi-storey parking, and a combined leisure and sports facility. The latter, known as Billingham Forum, opened in 1967 and contains a swimming pool, ice rink and a grade II listed theatre.

Sterling Organics, Sterling Place, Dudley,
Cramlington, Northumberland NE23
Designed by Ryder and Yates
Built 1972, not listed, P.098

↑ Gordon Ryder and Peter Yates formed their practice in 1953 in Newcastle having met while working together on Berthold Lubetkin's masterplan for Peterlee. Their influential body of work is predominantly located across the north-east of England. They were able to draw upon their previous experience at Killingworth (see Engineering Research Station for British Gas, below) when commissioned to design three buildings by Sterling Organics at their industrial complex. Each had a distinct function – one serving as a main entrance, one providing office space and the other a restaurant – but the brief demanded that all be capable of expansion if necessary. Connected by covered walkways, they form a cohesive group through the consistent use of pre-cast concrete panels in exposed white quartz aggregate. An internal courtyard is enclosed with glazed panels. The composition is lent a sculptural quality through the soaring cantilevered entrance canopy. Further artistic flourishes are found inside the entrance hall: Peter Yates's mural titled *Carbon Molecular Structures* depicts the molecular structure of paracetamol.

Cummins Engine Factory, Yarm Road,
Morton Palms, Darlington D1
Designed by Kevin Roche, John Dinkerloo and Associates
Built 1964–65, listed grade II*, P.079

↑ The second of two buildings for Cummins Engine Company (below), this rectangular single-storey building housed both office and workshop areas. Its primary function was to manufacture four engine components: fuel injectors, fuel pumps, air compressors and vibration dampers. The structural frame, with protruding 'I' beams at eaves level, is comprised of copper-coloured oxidising steel known as Cor-ten. The grey-tinted glazing is set into structural neoprene gaskets. The use of Cor-ten steel and neoprene gaskets was a first for a British building. The external areas, by the American landscape architect Daniel Urban Kiley, were added 1964–66 and are grade II listed.

Cummins Manufacturing Facility, Yarm Road,
Morton Palms, Darlington D1
Designed by James Cubitt and Partners
with Eero Saarinen and Associates
Built 1963–64, not listed, P.078

↑ One of two buildings commissioned by the Cummins Engine Company. According to a brief drawn up by the architect Kevin Roche, the first was to be a windowless box and the second a glass box (above). Once constructed, however, the first building did have windows albeit for 'psychological' reasons only: an artificial light factor of 75 lumens was maintained at all times. The building consists of a single-storey manufacturing area to the south of the site and a two-storey administrative block to the north. These are connected by a double-height canteen with kitchen facilities. The steel structural frame is visible externally, with infill being cavity brickwork stabilised with tension rods.

Darlington Town Hall, Feethams, Darlington DL1
Designed Williamson, Faulkner-Brown and Partners
Built 1967–70, not listed, P.080

↑ Unlike the civic centres erected in Newcastle and Middlesbrough (both below), in Darlington the 'Town Hall' moniker was retained and, in a further nod to tradition, the council chambers were arranged in the usual adversarial manner. It was commissioned in 1964 to consolidate the council's activities under one roof. Intended as part of a civic ensemble, the new town hall facade is comprised of intermittent vertical bands of reconstructed granite to mimic the upward thrust of the nearby St Cuthbert's church steeple. The abstract sculpture outside the town hall is by the artist John Hoskins and, titled *Resurgence*, symbolises the town's resurrection following the loss of industry in the 1960s.

Dunelm House, Durham University, New Elvet, Durham DH1
Designed by Michael Powers and Richard Raines
of Architects Co-Partnership
Built 1964–66, not listed, P.081

↑ Dunelm House was designed by Michael Powers, partner of the firm Architects Co-Partnership, with the assistance of Richard Raines, a graduate of the Architectural Association. Cut into the banks of the River Wear, the building houses university staffrooms and student clubrooms. Outdoor terraces, accessed from the dining and lounge areas, take advantage of the riverside location and also offer views of Kingsgate Bridge (below). Kitchen, staff and clubrooms are generally placed furthest from the river. Construction is off-form concrete, with care taken to achieve a high-standard finish. Robust detailing is also evidenced internally, with pivot doors enabling fussy jambs and architraves to be omitted.

Kingsgate Bridge, Durham University, Durham DH1
Designed by Ove Arup and Partners
Built 1963, listed grade I, P.082

↑ Spanning the River Wear, and linking the oldest and newest parts of Durham University, Kingsgate Bridge was the last structure designed by Sir Ove Arup himself. Born in Newcastle to Scandinavian parents, Arup was also responsible for Newcastle's Byker Viaduct (below). Kingsgate Bridge is a reinforced concrete structure, made with white cement and Shap granite, then grit blasted. To eliminate the need for scaffolding, the bridge was cast in two halves. Each half, supported by a slender truss, was mounted on a revolving cone either side of the river. Then, having been rotated through 90 degrees, the two halves were locked together with a simple bronze expansion joint.

St Aidan's College, Durham University,
Windmill Hill, Durham DH1
Designed by Sir Basil Spence and Partners
Built 1964, not listed, PP.084–085

↑ St Aidan's College was conceived as a residential and social campus, rather than a teaching facility, and is comprised of three buildings arranged around an inner courtyard. The main block to the north houses a double-height refectory, kitchen facilities and guest accommodation, while the staggered east and curved west wings are both residential blocks. A chapel was planned but never built. All structures are of reinforced concrete and load-bearing brick: the concrete vaulted arches are common to other buildings by Spence including Falmer House, University of Sussex (1962), Glasgow Airport (1966) and Hyde Park Cavalry Barracks (1970).

Trevelyan College, Durham University,
Elvet Hill Road, Durham DH1
Designed by Stillman and Eastwick-Field
Built 1965–67, not listed, P.083

↑ The college was designed to accommodate 250 female undergraduates in single study bedrooms, though some double rooms were included. To avoid the need for long corridors, the adopted plan was a series of interlocking hexagons, each with six bedrooms and its own service core. This naturally formed a series of inner courtyards and cloisters. Amenities such as the library, common rooms and dining hall enabled the college to host conferences and conventions outside of term. The structure is mainly reinforced concrete cast in situ, although a steel space frame supports the dining hall roof. External walls are faced in light grey handmade bricks.

Crowhall Towers, Crowhall Lane, Felling, Gateshead NE10
Designed by John Poulson
Built 1966–68, not listed, P.099

↑ Commissioned by Felling Urban District Council, Crowhall Towers is a housing scheme by the architect and business man John Poulson, who, despite never formally qualifying, designed several buildings including Leeds International Swimming Pool (1966) before being jailed for fraud in 1974. His scheme for Crowhall was originally made up of six 7-storey maisonette blocks containing 185 dwellings in total, alongside a 16-storey tower containing 88 dwellings with a public house at ground level. Four of the maisonette blocks were demolished in 1987.

Gateshead Police Station, High West Street, Gateshead NE8
Designed by Gateshead Borough Architects' Department (under Leslie Berry)
Built 1971–72, not listed, P.100

↑ A mostly four-storey structure, entry is via an open pedestrian footbridge at first-floor level. The building was commissioned by Gateshead Corporation on behalf of Durham Police Authority and overseen by the borough architect Leslie Berry. The structure is reinforced concrete with brick facings and deep recessed windows. The scheme is reminiscent of the many police stations designed by Lancashire County Council Architects' Department in the same period.

Hartlepool Civic Centre, Victoria Road, Hartlepool TS24
Designed by Clifford Culpin and Partners
Built 1973–76, not listed, P.089

↑ Along with the new market hall (1968) and shopping precinct (1971), Hartlepool Civic Centre was part of a central area redevelopment by Clifford Culpin and Partners. Four storeys high and constructed in red brick, the building contains offices, committee rooms with moveable partitions, the council chamber and police headquarters. The clean lines are somewhat disrupted by the glass and steel canopy at the main entrance, possibly a later addition.

Engineering Research Station for British Gas, Station Road, Killingworth, North Tyneside NE12
Designed by Ryder and Yates
Built 1966–7, listed grade II*, P.105

↑ Initially commissioned by British Gas to design a building for researching methods of producing gas, the discovery of natural gas under the North Sea switched the emphasis from production to distribution. The building, erected on the site of the former Killingworth Colliery and located close to Killingworth New Town, is three storeys high and rectangular on plan. Internally, the main building has two separate elements: a front section with car park and two levels of accommodation – the latter originally containing a library and canteen – and a rear section housing offices and laboratories, which if needed could be easily extended. Indeed the extension to house a restaurant and lecture theatre (1976) is also by Ryder and Yates. The main structure is reinforced concrete with pre-cast panels. The conical water tanks and cylindrical vents on the roof give the building its distinct appearance.

Church House, Grange Road, Middlesbrough TS1
Architect unknown
Built 1974, not listed, P.090

↑ Church House is so named having been constructed on the former site of a church hall. The 15-storey tower was erected by the property developer Yarmside Holdings and was initially used as a tax office; it is now multi-tenanted. The structural frame is reinforced concrete: hung pre-cast concrete panels minimised the need for scaffolding during construction.

Dorman Long Tower, South Bank Coke Ovens, Middlesbrough
Architect unknown
Built 1954–57, not listed, P.092

↑ Dorman Long Tower is a remnant of the South Bank Coke Ovens constructed by the specialist engineering firm of Otto Simon Carves. With a weekly throughput of 25,000 tons of coal, the concrete tower acted as a huge supply bunker for the since-demolished coke ovens.

Middlesbrough Civic Centre, off Albert Road, Middlesbrough TS1
Designed by Teesside County Borough Architects' Department (under JV Wall)
Built 1971–73, not listed, P.091

↑ With the establishment of the County Borough of Teesside in 1968, it was determined that its administrative centre should be located in Middlesbrough – a move which caused some consternation in the still-developing town of Billingham (see above). The existing grade II* listed town hall (1889), designed by the architect George Gordon Hoskins, required expanding to fulfil this new role. A new four-storey civic centre, linked via a pedestrian footbridge, was the solution. The building is brick cavity construction with aluminium-framed glazing. The steel and concrete structure is expressed externally, forming a colonnade at street level.

Byker Viaduct, Byker, Newcastle upon Tyne NE6
Designed by Ove Arup and Partners
Built 1976–79, not listed, P.102

↑ Constructed as part of the Byker redevelopment, the viaduct is an 815-metre-long curvilinear bridge designed by the engineering firm of Ove Arup and Partners to take the Newcastle Metro light rail system over the Ouseburn Valley and river towards Newcastle city centre. Byker Viaduct is noted for its innovative use of cantilevered sections of reinforced concrete, with counter-cast joints glued with an epoxy resin. The bridge won the Concrete Society Award for Civil Engineering in 1980.

Byker Wall, Byker Estate, Newcastle upon Tyne NE6
Designed by Ralph Erskine and Vernon Gracie
Built 1969–82, listed grade II*, P.101

↑ The Byker Wall forms part of the wider Byker redevelopment scheme, and remains one of the foremost examples of post-1945 social housing in Britain. It is noted for the architects' engagement with residents and user groups in reaching design decisions – a novel concept at the time. The estate is comprised of a mix of housing types. The continuous wall which bounds the estate to the north is, in places, eight storeys high. It houses 620 maisonettes and functions as a sound barrier, reducing traffic noise from the A193 bypass to South Shields. Construction is in situ cast concrete with concrete block and brick walls. Timber facings, balconies and ventilators are used to add flashes of colour to the exterior.

Claremont Complex, Newcastle University, Claremont Road, Newcastle upon Tyne NE1
Designed by Sheppard, Robson and Partners
Built 1965–68, not listed, P.104

↑ Located opposite Merz Court (1964), also by Sheppard, Robson and Partners, the Claremont Complex consists of several interconnected buildings constructed in phases. The first phase included the Building Science block (1965). At the heart of the complex is Claremont Tower, a 12-storey structure built to house the library and seminar rooms. Originally intended to be 20 storeys high, the tower was reduced at the insistence of the city planning authorities necessitating the construction of Claremont Bridge – a low-rise block spanning Claremont Road. Not only did this provide the necessary additional accommodation, but it also created a link with land earmarked for future university expansion. Completing the composition is the Fine Art Extension (1967) and the Daysh Building (1968), the latter housing the university's Department of Geography.

Hadrian Bridge, over Great North Road, Newcastle University, King's Road, Newcastle upon Tyne NE1
Designed by Newcastle City Engineers and Planning Department
Built 1975, not listed, P.106

↑ This single-storey concrete bridge, with viewing portholes to both sides, spans the Great North Road and connects the east side of the university campus with Robinson Library (below) to the west. At the time of construction, the Great Road North was being widened to create 'Central Motorway West', with the library site earmarked for a new court building. Designed by Napper Collerton, Newcastle Crown Court (1998) was eventually erected at Quayside.

Hadrian Building, Newcastle University, King's Road, Newcastle upon Tyne NE1
Designed by Sir William Whitfield
Built 1960–64, not listed, P.109

↑ Previously known as the King's Road Centre, the Hadrian Building adjoins the older Students' Union (1924) by Cackett, Burns, Dick and McKellar. It was built partly as an extension to the existing union building, and also to provide a new refectory for the university campus. An elevated block, known as the 'flying wing', housed two levels of union accommodation including games and music rooms with administrative functions above. The refectory, split over four levels, included a kitchen and bakery on level 1, self-service snack rooms on level 2 and main dining on level 3. The dance hall, which occupies the top-most level, was designed as an isolated element with the lower levels acting as a podium. Structurally, it has a reinforced concrete frame, and at podium level is faced with course-textured pre-cast concrete panels. The copper-roofed dance hall level is finished with polished grey granite.

Herschel Building, Newcastle University, Newcastle upon Tyne NE1
Designed by Basil Spence and Partners
Built 1957–62, not listed, P.107

↑ The Herschel Building was commissioned by the Physics Department of King's College, University of Durham, before becoming part of Newcastle University in 1963. The two main components of the original design were a two-storey and basement research block, with laboratories arranged around a top-lit central hall, and a six-storey teaching block with library and adjoining lecture theatres. After construction had commenced in 1957, predicted student numbers increased requiring an additional storey be added to both elements – a design change most evident with the research block. Prior to completion, Spence commissioned the artist Geoffrey Clarke, with whom he had previously collaborated with at Coventry Cathedral (1956–62), to provide a sculpture for the external courtyard. *Spiral Nebula* was intended to evoke the scientific advances of the period. The original waxed finish, however, was not to Spence's taste, so the sculpture was flame-blasted and painted grey.

Jesmond Library, St George's Terrace, Jesmond, Newcastle upon Tyne NE2
Designed by Harry Faulkner-Brown of Williamson, Faulkner-Brown and Partners
Built 1962–63, listed grade II, P.108

↑ Occupying a corner site, Jesmond Library is comprised of two main elements: a steel-framed drum-shaped structure which houses the main lending area, and a flat-roofed two-storey administrative block of grey brick. The lending area, with free-standing bookcases, is enclosed by a saw-tooth arrangement of external windows and panels of Balmoral red granite. Tubular steel columns at the perimeter support steel lattice girders to achieve a 17.5-metre clear span. The library was the recipient of a RIBA Bronze Medal in 1965, and is one of numerous libraries designed by Harry Faulkner-Brown (see Robinson Library, below).

Manors Car Park, Trafalgar Street, Newcastle upon Tyne NE1
Designed by Brims and Co
Built 1969, not listed, P.110

↑ Manors Car Park was part of Newcastle's chief planning officer Wilfred Burns's car-centric 1963 Development Plan to modernise the city and increase its economic appeal. With the A167(M) 'Central Motorway East' (1975) providing ease of access for vehicles, free parking also formed part of the strategy. Entered via a centralised ramp, the curved concrete multi-storey car park is almost sculptural; its form, however, was dictated by site constraints. The pedestrian footbridge which wraps around Swan House (below) connects the car park to the rest of the city centre.

MEA House, Ellison Place, Newcastle upon Tyne NE1
Designed by Ryder and Yates
Built 1972–74, listed grade II, P.111

↑ Taking ideas from both Berthold Lubetkin and the Swiss-born architect Le Corbusier, Ryder and Yates were keen to practise architecture for social service. Commissions for healthcare and welfare followed, including the Newcastle Men's Social Services Centre and Sunderland's Salvation Army Swan Lodge Lifehouse (below). MEA House was built to accommodate several charitable organisations under one roof. The name is derived from the design competition organised on behalf of its three benefactors: Mungo Campbell [M], Esther McCracken [E] and Alistair Fife [A]. In order to comply with height restrictions imposed by planners while housing all the required accommodation, Ryder and Yates produced a design which spanned an existing road to the north of the site. Neighbouring buildings including a college, YMCA and church formed a courtyard from which an entrance ramp is accessed. Eight storeys high with basement, the building has a steel frame with reinforced concrete cores. Mirrored glass was used externally, alongside easy-to-maintain brown brindle brick. Accommodation includes a hall and stage, a common room, and an internal courtyard and garden.

Newcastle Civic Centre, St Mary's Place,
Newcastle upon Tyne NE1
Designed by George Kenyon
Built 1956–1967, listed grade II*, P.103

↑ Set around a courtyard containing the artist David Wynne's *Swans in Flight*, the Civic Centre includes two four-storey blocks to the south and east, a civic suite and circular council chamber to the west, and a 12-storey block with tower and 25-bell carillon to north. The 12 bronze seahorses which top the carillon were sculpted by John Robert Murray McCheyne, while the statue mounted below is another work by Wynne titled *River God Tyne*. Also of note are two glazed murals in the rates hall by Victor Pasmore and the main entrance gates by Geoffrey Clarke. The structure is reinforced concrete throughout, with a rich variety of finishing materials deployed including Cornish granite and Broughton Moor stone.

Robinson Library, Newcastle University,
Jesmond Road West, Newcastle upon Tyne NE2
Designed by Harry Faulkner-Brown of Faulkner-Brown Hendy Watkinson Stonor
Built 1980–82, not listed, P.112

↑ In addition to Jesmond Library (above), Harry Faulkner-Brown designed a number of university libraries including those at Nottingham (1972), Loughborough (1979) and Newcastle's Robinson Library (1982). Considered a world authority on library design, Faulkner-Brown's 'ten commandments' were that libraries should be flexible, compact, accessible, extendible, organised, comfortable, constant in environment, secure, economic and provide varied reading material. Bounded by Great North Road to the west, this four-storey brick-faced building is connected to the rest of the university campus via Hadrian Bridge (above). Blank elevations act as an acoustic buffer to the motorway.

Salvation Army Men's Social Services Centre,
City Road, Newcastle upon Tyne NE1
Designed by Ryder and Yates
Built 1972–74, listed grade II, P.113

↑ At three storeys, the Salvation Army Men's Social Services Centre accommodated bedrooms on the ground and second floors with communal facilities, including a restaurant, on the first floor. Its curvilinear form, faced in smooth blue brindle brick (also used internally) was designed to be extended horizontally if needed. The modular glazing was also designed for flexibility, allowing bedroom units to be reduced from three to two as required. The building's most distinguishing feature is the entrance ramp and sculpted canopy; the latter an exaggerated version of that found at Lubetkin's Highpoint II, Highgate (1938) in the London Borough of Haringey, and a device previously deployed by the architects for Sterling Organics (above).

Shieldfield House, Barker Street,
Shieldfield, Newcastle upon Tyne NE2
Designed by Douglass Wise and Partners
Built 1967, not listed, P.114

↑ One of a pair of near-identical high-rise blocks commissioned by Newcastle upon Tyne County Borough Council, and designed by the firm of Douglass Wise and Partners – the other being the slightly taller Vale House (1968). Shieldfield House rises to 26 storeys and follows an H-plan arrangement with a circulation core on the north side. The core is faced with brickwork externally, a feature mimicked on the south elevation of this otherwise concrete-panelled edifice.

St James' Park, Barrack Road, Newcastle upon Tyne NE1
Designed by Faulkner-Brown Hendy Watkinson Stonor
Built 1972–73, not listed, PP.116–117

↑ Commissioned to prepare a plan for the redevelopment of St James' Park, the approach of the architects was not hugely different to that they took in the planning of university libraries (see Jesmond and Robinson libraries, above). Football stadia, they concluded, should be accessible, safe, compact, economic, etc. Particular to St James' Park, however, was the need for phased development and the continued use of the stadium while works were underway. Ultimately, only one phase was carried out and this was completed close season. The scheme retained the existing pitch-side terrace of the east stand, but added a grandstand with 20 further rows of terraced seating and concourses. Both the terracing and concourses are reinforced concrete. Exposed concrete is bush hammered externally and fairfaced inside. The roof is a 25-metre cantilevered steel structure, permitting unobstructed views.

Swan House, Pilgrim Street, Newcastle upon Tyne NE1
Designed by Robert Matthew, Johnson-Marshall and Partners
Built 1967–69, not listed, P.118

↑ Swan House was a commercial development originally tenanted by Post Office Telecommunications (later British Telecom) and named after Joseph Swan (1828–1914), a pioneer in developing electric lighting. Outside the building, a sculpture titled *Articulated Opposites* (1968) by the artist Raymond Arnott celebrates Swan's work. The building itself is comprised of two elements. The podium is an in situ cast concrete structure, faced with York stone, and provides three levels of office space. The larger elevated part of the building houses a further seven floors of office space, and was constructed from pre-cast concrete components. From the fourth floor, a pedestrian overpass links Swan House with Manors Car Park (see above).

Apollo Pavilion, Oakerside Drive, Peterlee, County Durham SR8
Designed by Victor Pasmore
Built 1969, listed grade II*, P.093

↑ Victor Pasmore's involvement with Peterlee began in 1954 with his appointment as consultant architectural designer to the new town's development committee: the departure of the architect Berthold Lubetkin from the original design team, along with financial difficulties, demanded fresh impetus. Pasmore's pavilion was intended as the focal point for the Sunny Blunts Housing Estate. A brook which divided housing to the north and south was dammed, with the pavilion effectively acting as a bridge over a newly formed lake. Murals on the north and south walls, having almost completely faded away, were reinstated during restoration works in 2009.

Steel House, former British Steel Complex,
Redcar, Cleveland TS10
Designed by Middleton, Fletcher and Partners
Built 1977, not listed, P.094

↑ Not dissimilar to Sunderland's Civic Centre (below), the design for Steel House by Middlesbrough-based Middleton, Fletcher and Partners was based on a series of interlocking hexagons and set in an open landscape. Six storeys high, the ground floor accommodated a lecture theatre, a restaurant and a shop, while the upper floors were mainly offices with plant equipment on the top floor.

Salvation Army Swan Lodge Lifehouse,
High Street East, Sunderland SR1
Designed by Ryder and Yates
Built 1982, not listed, PP.122–123

↑ Another building for the Salvation Army, Sunderland's Swan Lodge Lifehouse is a much more low-key building than some of Ryder and Yates's earlier buildings. Facing directly onto the street, it lacks the design flourishes such as the entrance canopy of the Men's Social Services Centre, Newcastle (above). It is comprised of two wings faced in smooth blue brindle brick with punched windows. The central core is set back from the street in order to soften the building's massing.

Sunderland Civic Centre, Burdon Road, Sunderland SR2
Designed by John Bonnington of Sir Basil Spence, Bonnington and Collins
Built 1965, not listed, PP.120–121

↑ Designed to fit on a sloping site, Sunderland Civic Centre is approached via a carefully arranged series of steps and ramps creating its own urban landscape. On plan, the building consists of two low-rise hexagonal blocks with inner courtyards, an administrative block to the south, and a connected car park to the north. All structures are faced externally in brindled brick and red tile giving cohesiveness to the whole. Internally, bespoke fitting and fixtures were designed by Bonnington, some adopting the hexagon as a motif.

Town Central Area, off Middle Street, Sunderland SR1
Designed by Llewelyn-Davies, Weeks and Partners
with Ian Frazer and Associates
Built 1967–69, not listed, P.119

↑ Sat above the Bridges Shopping Centre in Sunderland, these three 19-storey towers, each containing 90 individual dwellings, were commissioned by Sunderland County Borough Council. The structural frame is reinforced concrete with brick infill. Pre-cast concrete cills and headers lend some character to the elevations.

Edith Avenue, Washington, Tyne and Wear NE37
Designed by Napper, Errington, Collerton, Barnett and Allott
Built 1964–69, not listed, P.124

↑ Completed in 1969, the Edith Avenue development is made up of several three- to five-storey concrete-framed blocks, faced with brick. Nearly a third of the total 673 dwellings are at ground level with the rest being deck access; the five-storey blocks have lifts access also. Each block has its own designated parking area and semi-enclosed courtyard for sitting and play. The houses were built subsequent to Washington being designated a New Town in 1964. The practice was responsible for further housing schemes in Washington including the low-rise Sulgrave Village (1972).

Beacon House, Grenada Drive, Whitley Bay NE26
Designed by Ryder and Yates
Built 1962, not listed, P.125

↑ Beacon House is supposedly the first residential tower block constructed in the north-east of England, and was originally to be one of four similar towers. At 11 storeys high, it contains 44 individual dwellings, each with its own balcony. Like many of Ryder and Yates's later buildings, an extended canopy marks out the main entrance. A mural by Yates titled *Processions of Shells* adorns the entrance lobby wall. Construction is mostly reinforced concrete, with minimal brick infill beneath the extensive glazing.

Wilton Centre, Wilton, Redcar TS10
Designed by Building Design Partnership
Built 1975, not listed, P.095

↑ The Wilton Centre is an office development built for the chemical engineering company Imperial Chemical Industries, whose refineries were located nearby. Partially overlooking an artificial lake, the mainly three-storey blocks accommodated drawing offices and research and development laboratories and were arranged to create five enclosed courtyards. The seven stair towers add vertical thrust to the composition. Mostly faced in red brick with ribbon windows, the building was awarded a Certificate of Merit by the Brick Development Association in 1977.

Hexagon Tower, Delaunays Road, Blackley, Manchester M9
Designed by Richard Seifert and Partners
Built 1971, not listed, P.144

↑ As with London's Centre Point (1961–66) and Space House (1964–68), the design for Hexagon Tower by the commercially focused Richard Seifert and Partners made use of cruciform pre-cast concrete panels hung from a reinforced concrete frame. Although this minimised the need for scaffolding and speeded up construction, paradoxically the building was faced with labour-intensive tesserae. Built for the chemicals firm Imperial Chemical Industries, the podium and tower arrangement allowed for acoustic separation from the ground-level machine hall and the upper-level office spaces. The angular concrete motif of the external elevation was carried through into the main foyer, which featured a folded concrete plate ceiling, now obscured. A further three towers were planned for the site though never realised.

Chorley Police Station, St Thomas's Road, Chorley PR7
Designed by Lancashire County Council Architects' Department (under Roger Booth)
Built 1968, not listed, P.174

↑ Along with the Town Hall and Magistrates' Court, Chorley Police Station completes a civic ensemble grouped around a small courtyard. It is a seven-storey concrete-framed building whose cantilevers allowed for the inclusion of upper-level walkways and balconies while adding visual drama. Entry is gained via external stairs spanning a water feature. The neighbouring low-rise magistrates' court, with its distinctive pyramid roof lanterns, is also by Lancashire County Council Architects' Department. After Chorley, the department developed a method of concrete construction which utilised pre-cast elements. Known as Elemental Design Components, the system was used for police stations at Morecambe (1971), Wigan (1972) and Skelmersdale (1976).

Carlisle Civic Centre, Rickergate, Carlisle CA3
Designed by Charles B Pearson and Partners
Built 1964, not listed, P.166

↑ Following a design competition in 1957 which attracted 194 entries, Charles B Pearson and Partners emerged victorious with a three-part arrangement comprised of an 11-storey square office block, a low-rise rates hall and civic suite, and an elevated council chamber. The tower was constructed using pre-cast concrete components, while the quartzite floor and terrazzo counters of the rates hall were described as 'municipal, not commercial' after the building opened in March 1964. Of some interest is the rotunda which houses the council chamber: its shape reflected a desire to reduce separation between council members of opposing political persuasions. Reorganisation plans, subsequent to flood damage in 2015, call for the demolition of the rotunda, though the office block, rates hall and civic suite are likely to be retained.

Chaplaincy Centre, Lancaster University Campus, Bailrigg, Lancaster LA1
Designed by Cassidy and Ashton
Built 1969, not listed, P.168

↑ Unlike many planned campuses, Bridgewater, Shepheard and Epstein's plan for Lancaster University followed a different ethos in proposing a set of guiding principles for future growth rather than a rigid plan of future buildings. This approach negated the problem with many grand schemes of never quite reaching completion. The practice designed several of the campus's buildings including the library, sports centre, and computer and science blocks. The most visually striking building on campus, however, is the Chaplaincy Centre by the Preston-based firm Cassidy and Ashton. In keeping with moves toward greater ecumenical co-operation, as enshrined in the 1969 Shared Churches Act, this single chaplaincy was intended for use by all Christian denominations. At the insistence of the Roman Catholic Diocese of Lancaster, a chapel separate to that used by Anglicans and Nonconformists was provided. Nonetheless, moveable glazed screens meant that both chapels could be opened on to the central area for shared activities such as carol services. The three spires which rise above the space indicate a coming together of the three denominations.

Forton Services, White Carr Lane, Lancaster LA2
Designed by Bill Galloway and Ray Anderson of TP Bennett and Son
Built 1964–65, listed grade II, P.167

↑ Indicative of Britain's embrace of the motor vehicle in the 1960s, Forton Services was commissioned by Top Rank Motor Inns as the Preston By-pass was absorbed by the M6 motorway. Located between junctions 32 and 33, the services themselves are not of great interest: two flat-roofed buildings connected by a pedestrian footbridge over the carriageway. What distinguishes them, however, is the instantly recognisable former Pennine Tower. A cantilevered restaurant and sun deck once occupied the head of this hexagonal concrete structure which, at 22 metres in height, afforded diners views over the surrounding countryside. Sadly, the restaurant closed in 1989.

Dental School, The Royal Liverpool University Hospital, Prescot Street, Liverpool L7
Designed by Holford Associates
Built 1963–78, not listed, P.128

↑ Part of The Royal Liverpool University Hospital (see below), the dental school was completed to the designs of Anthony Clark Partnership.

Department of Electrical Engineering and Electronics, University of Liverpool, Ashton Street, Liverpool L69
Designed by Yorke Rosenberg Mardall
Built 1962–65, not listed, P.129

↑ A signature of the firm of Yorke Rosenberg Mardall, as exemplified by the Department of Electrical Engineering and Electronics, University of Liverpool, was the use of white ceramic tiles. This was inspired by Le Corbusier's Armée du Salut (1929) in Paris and the General Institute of Pensions (1934) in Prague designed by Josef Havlíček and Karel Honzík; the latter of which Rosenberg had been involved with early in his career. The ground floor of the main six-storey block is fully glazed, with ribbon windows and stack bond tiling to the upper floors. Access is via a footbridge over a small moat.

Fire Training Centre, Storrington Avenue, Liverpool L11
Designed by Hall, O'Donahue and Wilson with Ronald Bradbury
Built 1967, not listed, P.130

↑ Erected on a former drill yard of Storrington Avenue Fire Station, the training centre was designed to enable firemen to train fighting actual fires. Thus, access to all four sides of the building had to be maintained. Teaching and administrative functions were placed at the rear of the building, with dining and recreational facilities facing on to Storrington Avenue. It was intended that three storeys of sleeping accommodation be built above the latter, and foundations were designed accordingly. However, the Home Office's unwillingness to provide funding meant that these, and a planned gymnasium, were omitted from the final design. Of note is the limited amount of timber used for the roof structure: building collapse, resulting from simulated fires, had to be avoided. Similarly, the flat concrete roof of the fire house lacked finishing materials which might be flammable. By necessity, therefore, it leaked. The brick stair tower, while providing vertical circulation, also allowed evacuation procedures to be practised.

Kingsway Tunnel Vents, Waterloo Road, Liverpool L3 / Ferry View Road, Wallasey CH44
Designed by Edmund Nuttall Limited
Built 1966–71, not listed, P.131

↑ At either end of the Kingsway Tunnel, connecting Liverpool and the Wirral, are two near-identical vents. Each features a low-rise dark grey brick structure above which rises a concrete chimney and two sculptural air-intake ducts: the Kingsway Tunnel is twin-bore, so each duct ventilates a single tunnel. One subtle difference between the two vents is the raking pipes which connect to the central chimney. On the Wirral side these are square-sectioned, whereas on the Liverpool side they are cylindrical.

Liverpool Metropolitan Cathedral of Christ the King,
Mount Pleasant, Liverpool L35
Designed by Frederick Gibberd
Built 1962–67, listed grade II*, P.132

↑ Having taken the decision to abandon Edwin Lutyen's costly interwar designs for the Metropolitan Cathedral, the Diocese of Liverpool announced an architectural competition which attracted 258 entries, including those from architects such as Denys Lasdun, the Smithsons, and the Archigram group. Emerging as the winner, in 1960, was Frederick Gibberd, whose proposal was heavily influence by Oscar Niemeyer's design for the Cathedral of Brasilia (1958–1970). Another source of inspiration was Gerard Goalen's Church of Our Lady of Fatima in Harlow; Gibberd had acted as architect planner for the new town and was present at the church's opening. A circular plan was adopted, though Gibberd did consider elliptical and octagonal options; the latter made manifest at Hopwood Hall Chapel, Middleton (below). Sixteen reinforced concrete flying buttresses support the prefabricated concrete panels of the roof cone and the vertical ribs of the tower. Between each of the ribs is a series of glass and concrete panels designed by John Piper and Patrick Reytiens. Other noted artwork includes the marble floor in the nave by David Atkins, and the carved Portland stone crosses above the elaborate main entrance doors by William Mitchell.

Queen Elizabeth II Law Courts, Derby Square, Liverpool L2
Designed by Pat Duffy with Farmer and Dark
Built 1979–84, not listed, P.133

↑ Liverpool's Queen Elizabeth II Law Courts were designed by Pat Duffy, principal architect within the Property Services Agency's Directorate of Civil Accommodation, in consultation with the practice of Farmer and Dark. The 28 courtrooms were designed to hear High, Crown and County Court work. It is a reinforced concrete structure with non-loadbearing pre-cast concrete panels, ribbed with exposed aggregate.

Former headquarters of Royal Insurance,
Old Hall Street, Liverpool L69
Designed by Tripe and Wakeham Partnership
Built 1974–76, not listed, P.134

↑ Not to be confused with the neo-baroque Royal Insurance Building (1903) by James F Doyle, this 13-storey building was built as the new headquarters of the insurer. Typical of an era where pre-cast concrete was deployed in a non-structural capacity, it was clad in pale orange-coloured panels and, unsurprisingly, was referred to by locals as 'The Sandcastle'. For the historian Sir Nikolaus Pevsner, however, its slit windows gave it the air of a fortress, again unsurprising for a firm whose recent commissions included the since-demolished Chelsea Barracks (1963), Westminster, London.

The Royal Liverpool University Hospital,
Prescot Street, Liverpool L7
Designed by Holford Associates
Built 1963–78, not listed, P.135

↑ Originally designed as a medical training centre, facilities included a central teaching school, lecture theatre, staff residences, an 800-bed ward and a dental school (above). Among the first buildings to be erected was the teaching school, a robust concrete structure presently known as the Linda McCartney Building, and a high-rise residential tower since demolished. Delays in construction meant the hospital did not fully open until 1978. The main hospital building is comprised of a low-rise podium containing outpatient services, above which rises a 12-storey ward block. Linked to it is the clinical sciences block and lecture theatre. These later buildings are of smooth-faced concrete components with ribbed concrete panels used for external stair cores.

Sculptural Wall at Knowsley Heights,
Primrose Drive, Huyton, Liverpool L36
Designed by Antony Holloway
Built 1962, not listed, P.136

↑ Antony Holloway is, perhaps, somewhat overshadowed by the artist William Mitchell, his one-time colleague at London County Council, where both were employed as design consultants in the 1950s. However, he is well regarded in the city of Manchester for the five stained-glass windows he designed for Manchester Cathedral, and for the Sculptural Wall (1968) which bounds the University of Manchester's North Campus. While his Manchester wall is listed grade II, this earlier example in Huyton, Liverpool, is not. At a length of 600 feet in length, it was claimed to be the largest wall of its kind to be built since the Middle Ages. As well as being decorative, it also acts as a retaining structure to three 11-storey tower blocks.

Sports and Fitness Centre, University of Liverpool,
Bedford Street North, Liverpool L69
Designed by Denys Lasdun and Partners
Built 1963–66, not listed, P.139

↑ Opened on 3 December 1966, the Sports and Fitness Centre accommodated a 33-metre swimming pool and a large sports hall designed for multiple uses including basketball, tennis and, it is claimed, Britain's first climbing wall: the pattern of reliefs in brick and concrete were designed by Donald Norman Mill, an associate of Lasdun's practice. The two major elements of the building are positioned either side of a central core which houses squash courts and provides access to a spectator gallery overlooking the pool. On the north- and south-facing elevations, raking pre-stressed pre-cast concrete columns support the roof.

Sydney Jones Library, University of Liverpool,
Chatham Street, Liverpool L7
Designed by Andrew Merrylees and Humphrey Sharpe
of Spence, Glover and Ferguson
Built 1974–76, not listed, P.137

↑ After winning the competition to design the new Coventry Cathedral (1951–62), the nationwide expansion in higher education provided Sir Basil Spence's practice with a rich seam of onward work. A masterplan for the University of Edinburgh was prepared in 1954, along with a science campus for the University of Nottingham (1955) and an expansion plan for the University of Southampton (1956). Building commissions often followed: at the University of Sussex, the firm designed a library of red brick and shuttered concrete, now listed grade II*. The Sydney Jones Library for the University of Liverpool bears some similarity with the Sussex library, being a reinforced concrete structure with brick facings. It is a four-storey structure, square on plan, with a central spine providing vertical circulation.

Tate & Lyle Sugar Silo, Regent Road, Kirkdale, Liverpool
Designed by David Bailey of Tate & Lyle Engineering Department
Built 1955–57, listed grade II*, P.138

↑ This single-chambered structure was designed to store 100,000 tons of raw sugar for use by Tate & Lyle's Love Lane refinery. It is comprised of 12 sections of in situ cast concrete supported by six external ribs, with access to the cavernous vaulted interior provided on both gables. Advancements in container shipping led to the development of a container port north of the Huskisson Dock, which, along with the closure of the refinery in 1981, led to the abandonment of the silo.

Barnes Wallis Building/Wright Robinson Hall, University of Manchester, North Campus (formerly UMIST), Manchester M1
Designed by WA Gibbons of Cruickshank and Seward
Built 1963–66, not listed, P.145

↑ Named after the scientist and engineer responsible for the invention of the bouncing bomb, the Barnes Wallis Building is one of several buildings commissioned in 1962 which would come to shape the University of Manchester's North Campus. The Barnes Wallis moniker refers specifically to the podium which once housed the campus's refectory and Students' Union. Wright Robinson Hall is the 15-storey tower which rises above the podium and, although part of a unified structure of white board-marked concrete, it was named separately to reflect its use as a hall of residence. A roof lantern, which brings light into the stair core, lends the tower its distinctive appearance.

Church of the Ascension, Royce Road, Hulme, Manchester M15
Designed by Robert Maguire and Keith Murray
Built 1970, not listed, P.146

↑ This Anglican church was designed by Robert Maguire and Keith Murray, key members of the New Churches Research Group, who, through buildings such as St Paul's, Bow Common (1958–60), gave form to the liturgical renewal which resonated throughout Britain in the second half of the 20th century. Church of the Ascension responded to the yet-to-be-completed (and now demolished) Hulme Crescents (1968–72) with a complex roof design. Maguire reasoned that, for the tenants of the Crescents, the roof would be the most common view of the church and, therefore, required due architectural treatment, unlike the external walls, which are of plain buff blockwork. Internally, free-standing columns support a succession of concrete ring beams, each in turn rotated 45 degrees to create an elaborate roof structure with a glazed central portion.

CIS Tower, Miller Street, Manchester M60
Designed by Gordon S Hay with Sir John Burnet, Tait and Partners
Built 1959–62, listed grade II, P.147

↑ The 25-storey CIS Tower was built as the headquarters of the Co-operative Insurance Society. The design was heavily influenced by the work of Skidmore, Owings and Merrill, notably the Inland Steel Building (1958) in Chicago, and a similar tower and podium arrangement was adopted. The building is steel-framed with glass curtain walls with anodised aluminium supports. Black-vitreous-enamelled-steel blanking panels mark out the individual storeys, while the tower's concrete service shaft, originally clad in centimetre-square, grey tesserae, is now covered by photovoltaic panels. Interior spaces, including the two executive-floor levels, were designed by Misha Black and Alexander Gibson of the Design Research Unit. The fibreglass mural which dominates the entrance lobby is by the artist William Mitchell.

Domestic and Trades College, Old Hall Lane, Fallowfield, Manchester M14
Designed by Derek B Hill for Manchester City Architects' Department (under Leonard C Howitt)
Built 1958–60, listed grade II, P.155

↑ The Domestic and Trades College, affectionately referred to as the 'Toastrack' by Mancunians owing to its striking form, was one of several technical colleges built across Manchester, and indeed Britain, as further education provision was expanded in the two decades following the Second World War. The design adheres to stringent guidelines set out by the Ministry of Education in a document titled 'Building Bulletin No.5' (1951), and consists of an administrative building, an eight-storey teaching tower and a workshop block. Made up of 23 reinforced concrete arches designed by the engineering firm LG Mouchel and Partners, the tapered form of the teaching tower was adopted to accommodate the wide diversity of functions within. Lecture theatres, laboratories and a bakery occupied the lower levels, while smaller rooms, mostly classrooms, were placed above. The building is presently unoccupied.

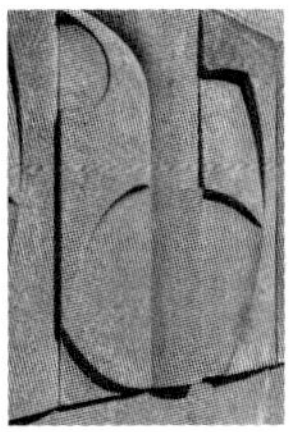

Ellen Wilkinson Humanities Building, University of Manchester, Blyton Street, Manchester M15
Designed by George Grenfell-Baines of Building Design Partnership
Built 1964, not listed, P.148

↑ This scheme by George Grenfell-Baines, founder of Building Design Partnership, was originally known simply as the Humanities Building and was comprised of two five-storey and one two-storey pinkish-grey concrete blocks arranged around a small courtyard. A paean to the structural and sculptural possibilities offered by concrete, bush-hammered columns reveal the Derbyshire gravel aggregate, while the moulded panels were designed in collaboration with the artist William Mitchell. The seven-storey teaching block is a later addition.

Extension to John Dalton Building, Manchester Metropolitan University, Oxford Road, Manchester M15
Designed by SAB Heppell for Manchester City Architects' Department
Built 1974, not listed, P.149

↑ John Dalton College of Technology first opened in 1964 and, designed by Derek B Hill, followed a similar plan arrangement to the Toastrack (above). In 1970, the college became a faculty of Manchester Polytechnic and, four years later, a five-storey steel-framed structure facing onto Oxford Road was erected to provide additional teaching and administrative accommodation. Pre-cast concrete units with exposed aggregate were suspended from the steel frame, with angled opaque glazing providing infill. Given the modest elevational treatment of the original building, it can be conjectured that this more visually assertive extension was always planned. The building is now part of Manchester Metropolitan University.

Manchester Oxford Road Station, Station Approach off Oxford Road, Manchester M1
Designed by William R Headley and Max Clendinning with Hugh Tottenham
Built 1960, listed grade II, P.151

↑ Set back from Oxford Road and occupying a slightly elevated position, the entrance hall and ticket offices of Manchester Oxford Road Station sit within an innovative segmented conoidal roof of laminated timber. An earlier example of such a structure, albeit in concrete, was that of the College of Building workshops (1957) by Manchester City Architects' Department, since demolished. The brick viaducts at Oxford Road, however, were deemed incapable of supporting anything too heavy, hence the appointment of Hugh Tottenham of the Timber Development Association as consultant engineer by Clendinning. The pair were also responsible for the platform structures, which were pre-formed in the joinery workshops before being erected on-site. Clendinning continued to experiment in laminate timber, designing his Maxima range of furniture in 1965.

Maths and Social Sciences Building, University of Manchester, North Campus (formerly UMIST), Manchester M1
Designed by WA Gibbons of Cruickshank and Seward
Built 1968, not listed, P.150

↑ Although more simplistic in form than either the Barnes Wallace Building (above) or the Renold Building (below), it is the Maths and Social Sciences Building that many people will most closely identify with the campus owing to the illuminated signage which once adorned the building. Mounted at the head of the 15-storey white concrete tower, the letters 'U-M-I-S-T' were clearly visible from the Mancunian Way below. Completing the composition to the east of the tower, and also of white concrete, is a simple low-rise lecture block.

Precinct Centre, University of Manchester, Oxford Road, Manchester M13
Designed by Wilson and Womersley
Built 1970–72, not listed, P.152

↑ After Hugh Wilson was appointed to masterplan an area along Oxford Road as part of Manchester's post-1945 higher education expansion, he invited Sheffield's city architect Lewis Womersley to join him and together they formed the architectural practice of Wilson Womersley. In Manchester, the pair would gain notoriety for their designs for the now-demolished Hulme Crescents (1968–72) and the much-criticised Arndale Centre (1972–79). Only slightly less controversial was their design for the Precinct Centre, a multi-storey, mixed-use development in red brick which connected with the University of Manchester's Business School via a footbridge over Oxford Road. The shops in the precinct struggled with students returning home during the summer months. Recent redevelopment work has seen the footbridge removed, and retail units relocated to the ground floor of the Business School.

Renold Building, University of Manchester,
North Campus (formerly UMIST), Manchester M1
Designed by WA Gibbons of Cruickshank and Seward
Built 1960–62, not listed, P.153

↑ This is another white concrete building designed by WA Gibbon of the Manchester-based firm of Cruickshank and Seward (see Barnes Wallis Building/Wright Robinson Hall above). Its purpose was to house multiple lecture theatres and seminar rooms. The faceted glazing to the east elevation of the tower gives the Renold Building its distinct identity, while the predominantly glazed staircase which protrudes on the north side of the building provides glimpses of activity and movement within. A wall painting, *Metamorphosis* (1968) by the artist Victor Pasmore, can be found in the entrance lobby.

St Augustine RC Church, Grosvenor Square,
Chorlton-upon-Medlock, Manchester M15
Designed by Desmond Williams Associates
Built 1967–68, listed grade II, P.154

↑ Considering the wave of novel church forms that prevailed throughout Europe during the 20th century, St Augustine, internally at least, conforms to tradition. This building is on an east–west axis, with seating either side of a central aisle and an altar occupying the west end. Above the altar there is the ceramic relief sculpture *Christ in Glory* by the artist Robert Brumby. The solid brick walls, punctuated only by the tall, narrow dalle de verre windows on the north and south elevations, engender a sense of sanctuary within the central worship space. The windows were designed by the noted glass artist Pierre Fourmaintraux.

Hopwood Hall Chapel, Oaken Bank Road, Middleton M24
Designed by Sir Frederick Gibberd
Built 1964–65, listed grade II, P.156

↑ Designed by Sir Frederick Gibberd in association with the Manchester- and Nottingham-based firm of Reynolds and Scott, Hopwood Hall Chapel was commissioned by the De La Salle Brothers, a Roman Catholic educational order. This octagonal building has a reinforced concrete frame with concrete block external walls. The lantern which rises above the copper-clad roof is comprised of exposed, pre-cast concrete ribs with coloured glass infill designed by David Atkins, a member of Gibberd's practice. The chapel bears some similarity with Gibberd's Liverpool Metropolitan Cathedral (above), which also featured work by Atkins.

Oldham Civic Centre, West Street, Oldham OL1
Designed by Cecil Howitt and Partners
Built 1975–77, not listed, P.157

↑ Designs for the Civic Centre were drawn up in 1960 and the building was constructed in two phases. The first phase, a low-rise structure built to accommodate housing and social services, was completed in 1962. Construction of the 15-storey reinforced concrete tower proceeded in 1975, and officially opened in 1977, allowing the council to move staff from the old town hall building. Reflecting Cold War tensions which existed at the time, the new building incorporated a nuclear bunker to protect senior staff members in the event of an attack.

Classroom at Kennington Primary School,
Kennington Road, Fulwood, Preston PR2
Designed by Ben Stephenson and Mike Bracewell under county architect Roger Booth, for Lancashire County Council Architects' Department
Built 1973–74, listed grade II, P.171

↑ Nicknamed 'The Bubble' by pupils and connected to the school's main building by a flat-roofed resource area, the classroom is comprised of 35 reinforced white polyester panels sat on a concrete base. It is believed to be the first fully structural plastic building constructed in Britain, and was a prototype for the intended mass production of glass fibre-reinforced plastic schools by Lancashire County Council Architects' Department. However, no further examples were built.

Preston Central Bus Station and Car Park,
Tithebarn Street, Preston PR1
Designed by Keith Ingham and Charles Wilson
of Building Design Partnership
Built 1968–69, listed grade II, P.169

↑ Central Bus Station was erected ahead of an expansion plan that foresaw a doubling of Preston's population. Ambitions to integrate Preston with Leyland and Chorley, in what would be named Central Lancashire New Town, ultimately foundered, though rising passenger numbers warranted provision of a substantial car park. The main structure is rectangular on plan with split-level decking either side of a central spine. Occupying the spine are passenger facilities such as information and booking offices, a café, rest rooms and kiosks. The double-height waiting areas at ground level include original features such as hardwood handrails and seating set against a black Pirelli rubber floor, and bespoke signage and clocks. In 2012, Preston City Council announced that the building would be demolished for financial reasons. However, in 2013 it was granted listed building status partly owing to the innovative use of reinforced plastic mouldings in casting the sculptural concrete decks.

Preston Guild Hall, Lancaster Road, Preston PR1
Designed by Robert Matthew Johnson Marshall and Partners
Built 1969–73, not listed, P.170

↑ Having been commissioned to design the hall in advance of the Preston Guild of 1972, labour strikes meant that the building wasn't completed until 1973. Above the brick-clad arcade of shops at ground level, concrete cantilevers support a concert hall theatre which can be accessed from an internal atrium. The building is one of a number of major developments, including St George's Shopping Centre (1966) and Preston Central Bus Station and Car Park (see above), which reflected Preston's growing regional significance. Indeed, the Guild Hall is connected to the bus station via an enclosed pedestrian footbridge.

College Bank Estate, College Bank Way, Rochdale OL12
Designed by Derek Broadbent
of Rochdale County Borough Council
Built 1965–70, not listed, P.158

↑ Known locally as the Seven Sisters, the flats at College Bank Way included four 21-storey blocks containing 476 dwellings and a further three 17-storey blocks of 286 dwellings. Designed by Derek Broadbent, borough architect and planning officer, each tower has a frame of reinforced concrete faced in dark brick, and was finished to a high standard in order to attract professionals. Individual murals adorn the entrance lobbies. Plans to demolish Town Mill Brow, Mitchell Hey, Tentercroft and Dunkirk Rise will leave just three of the sisters remaining: Holland Rise, Underwood and Mardyke.

Ormskirk Street United Reformed Church,
Ormskirk Street, St Helens WA10
Designed by Martin Purdy and Peter Bridges
Built 1976, not listed, P.141

↑ Ormskirk Street United Reformed Church is one of several places of worship designed by Purdy and Bridges, which combine secular function with worship in a manner first explored by the pair at the since-demolished Anglican church of St Philip and St James, Hodge Hill (1968). Another example is the Skelmersdale Ecumenical Centre (1973). Ormskirk Street URC is a three-storey building of brick and concrete construction with a tent-like roof structure that is redolent of the experimental churches of the Swiss architect Rainer Senn.

Former headquarters of Pilkington Glass,
Alexandra Works, Borough Road, St Helens WA10
Designed by Edwin Maxwell Fry of Fry, Drew and Partners
Built 1959–63, listed grade II, P.140

↑ Purpose-built as the new headquarters of Pilkington Glass, this complex of buildings sits within a landscape which Edwin Maxwell Fry designed in collaboration with the noted landscape architect Peter Youngman. The buildings, which include a museum and a canteen, vary in height from single storey up to 13 storeys, and feature a variety of glass finishes aimed at showcasing the firm's products. They are mostly concrete-framed with aluminium-framed windows. In the canteen, an abstract mural by the artist Victor Pasmore decorates the wall.

Stopford House, Piccadilly, Stockport SK1
Designed by JS Rank
Built 1975, not listed, P.159

↑ John S Rank was a senior figure within Harlow Development Corporation before taking up the role of director of development and town planning in Stockport around 1955. He was responsible for a number of buildings in the county including Hanover Tower and Pendlebury Towers (1968–69) on Lancashire Hill, Stockport. At 105 metres in length, the monolithic Stopford House was built to enable Stockport Metropolitan Borough Council to consolidate its various activities under one roof. Typical of the experimentation in finishing techniques prevalent at the time, the building displays bush-hammered, smooth and ribbed concrete, with an aggregate which is respectful of Sir Alfred Brumwell Thomas's nearby Town Hall (1908).

Lancastrian Hall and Central Library,
Chorley Road, Swinton M27
Designed by Leach, Rhodes and Walker
Built 1968, not listed, P.163

↑ One of the most recognisable buildings in Swinton, Lancastrian Hall and Central Library opened in 1970. The hall was intended for civic and community meetings, wedding receptions and election counts. Thus, the interior was designed to be as open as possible in order to promote flexibility. The expressive massing of the building, achieved through concrete cantilevers, is not essential and can be read as a playful gesture by the Manchester-based firm of Leach, Rhodes and Walker. The building has been closed to the public since 2015.

Swinton Civic Centre, Chorley New Road, Swinton M27
Designed by Cruickshank and Seward
Built 1973, not listed, PP.160–161

↑ This unremitting four-storey building is made up of repeat pre-cast concrete panels, and is connected to Sir Percy Thomas and Ernest Prestwich's Town Hall (1938) by an enclosed pedestrian walkway. Some visual interest is provided by an artificial cut in the external ground level which allowed the introduction of tapered columns – a reference, perhaps, to Le Corbusier's influential Unité d'Habitation (1952) in Marseille.

St Jude RC Church, Poolstock Lane, Worsley Mesnes, Wigan WN3
Designed by LAG Prichard and Son
Built 1964–65, listed grade II, P.176

↑ With previous experience of designing churches for the Roman Catholic Diocese of Liverpool including Our Lady of Perpetual Succour, Speke (1958) and Our Lady Queen of Peace, Litherland (1960), LAG Prichard and Son were instructed in 1964 to draw up plans for a new church on the expanding Worsley Mesnes Estate. The resulting design is an imposing fan-shaped church whose concrete frame radiates outwards from the east wall. Internally, the plan arrangement reflected recent liturgical thinking by offering uninterrupted views of the altar and white marble sanctuary. The mosaic behind the altar depicts Christ on the Cross and is by Hans Unger and Eberhard Schulz of the Unger Mosaic Workshop. Either side of the nave are six dalle de verre windows designed by the Liverpool artist Robin Riley. A circular brick baptistery replete with dalle de verre clerestory glazing, also by Riley, sits separately from the main church.

Wigan Civic Centre, Millgate, Wigan WN1
Designed by Percy Thomas Partnership
Built 1970, not listed, P.175

↑ Wigan Corporation's association with the long-established practice of Welsh architect Sir Percy Thomas began in the mid-1950s when they commissioned him, along with the architect Ernest Prestwich, to design their new Town Hall; previous experience included Swinton Town Hall (1938) and Tunbridge Wells Civic Centre (1939), both in a polite interwar style. Ill health forced Thomas to retire in 1963, though his practice was retained to masterplan a new town centre civic ensemble. The Civic Centre was completed under the direction of Norman Percy Thomas, Thomas's son, and is a four-storey structure mostly faced with smooth pre-cast concrete components, though the end stair core is ribbed.